ATLAS ARKHIVE FIVE
A MAMMAL'S NOTEBOOK

ATLAS ARKHIVE FIVE

EDITED BY ORNELLA VOLTA

COLLECTED WRITINGS OF

TRANSLATIONS BY ANTONY MELVILLE

DOCUMENTS OF THE AVANT-GARDE

A MAMMAL'S NOTEBOOK

erik satie

ATLAS PRESS LONDON

ATLAS ARKHIVE
DOCUMENTS OF
THE AVANT-GARDE
NUMBER 5 ERIK SATIE

Editor of this issue
Ornella Volta

Series Editors:
Alastair Brotchie
Malcolm Green
Antony Melville
Terry Hale
Chris Allen

Published by Atlas Press,
London WCIN 3XX.
Texts ©1996, Pierre Joseph-Lafosse, Ornella Volta and
Atlas Press
Illustrations © 1996,
Archives de la Fondation
Erik Satie.
Printed in the UK
by The Bath Press.
A CIP record for this book is available from the
British Library.
ISBN 0 947757 92 9

THE ATLAS ARKHIVE SERIES. The Arkhive series exists to examine and publish previously unavailable material relating to issues, neglected groups and pivotal figures, within the avant-garde "anti-tradition" of the last 100 years. Where possible each volume takes a documentary format, being either anthologies based on collections assembled by the groups themselves, or co-edited with the participation of members.

The first four issues, on *Dada Berlin*; *French Symbolist Literature*; *Georges Bataille & Acéphale*; and *Fluxus/Nouveau Réalisme* are still available; and these, along with forthcoming issues, are described at the end of this book.

ACKNOWLEDGEMENTS. I wish to thank Comte Henri de Beaumont and M. Jacques Guérin; and the late Mesdames Louise Leiris and Geneviève Seydoux, and Messieurs Robert Caby, Max Fontaine, Henry Kahnweiler, Jacques Lambert and Henri Sauguet, for the unpublished documents they have kindly allowed me to use. Thanks also to M. Gérald Hugon of Editions Max Eschig, and M. Hervé Burckel de Tell of Editions Salabert, for their permission to publish literary extracts from the scores by Erik Satie of which they are the respective publishers.
Ornella Volta

ATLAS PRESS would like to thank the Arts Council of England and the French Ministère des Affaires Etrangères (Burgess programme) for their grants towards this publication, which would not have been possible without their assistance.

Funded by
THE
ARTS
COUNCIL
OF ENGLAND

Tous droits réservés — même pour la Lune

Overleaf: *Erik Satie in his days as "The Velvet Gentleman," c. 1895/6.*

Erik Satie was endowed with a magical imagination, but was devoted to the strictest precision; he was always ready with the keenest of witticisms, but had a natural bent towards mysticism; he was an admirer of *plain chant*, but forever on the look-out for new musical forms. Seventy one years after his death, he is looked down on by some, worshipped by others, and is by no means done with questioning us, or arousing passionate arguments.

He never adhered to any "movement"; indeed he vigorously proclaimed "the independence of *his* aesthetic." Yet at different times a wide range of schools including Symbolism, Cubism, Neo-Classicism, Dada, Surrealism, conceptual art, repetitive music, minimalism, Fluxus, New Age, and Ambient music, have seen him as one of theirs.

His personality went well beyond the field of music, and he has been claimed as a nephew of Lewis Carroll, a younger cousin of Alphonse Allais, Alfred Jarry's foster-brother, an emulator of the Good Soldier Schweik, and a precursor of Ionesco. Satie preferred to present himself as "a man in the manner of Adam (he of Paradise)"; but did add to his spiritual genealogy by aligning himself with Edgar Allan Poe: "My humour," he said, "is reminiscent of Cromwell's. I am also indebted to Christopher Columbus, as the American spirit has sometimes tapped me on the shoulder, and I have joyfully felt its ironically icy bite."

Beau Brummel only considered himself perfectly elegant, when no one noticed the fact; Satie stood out as unique by suppressing any subjective indulgence. One will never learn from this "amnesic mammal's" autobiography anything more personal than his undoubtedly heroic struggle to have his disturbing contributions accepted by a rigid society. Satie has always disturbed people, as much in recent years as in his lifetime, but not always for the same reasons. Some of his inventions, which at the time were considered completely preposterous, such as his "prepared" piano, the booklet he had printed entirely in lower case, or the music he asked people "not to listen to," have since become common coin. But his role continues to be more than merely that of a precursor. Satie still seems, even now, contemporary, because the problems he brought to light remain unresolved.

Satie once compared himself to "that splendid bird" Strawinsky, describing himself as "a fish." He certainly lived on music as a fish lives in water. He owed all his pleasures, joys, discoveries, private jokes, and his fondest memories, to his activity as a "phonometrographer."

Yet he was aware (and probably suffered from it more than anyone else) of the limits of musical communication — fixed, as he noted, at one extreme by the existence of "the deaf." Like a Robinson Crusoe on his desert island, in need of not just one, but several Man Fridays, he was constantly looking to widen the range of people to whom he could address himself. Balancing dangerously on the wire of his humour, by turns tender and explosive, he ranged

Etude pour un buste de M. Erik SATIE (peint par lui-même)

from airy poems to down to disenchanted reflections, threatening epistles to wryly ironic talks, friendly "little notes" to peculiar advertisements, devastating aphorisms to enigmatic graphics.

The range of publications through which he managed to transmit his "messages in a bottle" included, among others: a Montmartre cabaret publication *(Le Chat Noir)*, an esoteric monthly *(Le Coeur)*, a modest suburban newspaper *(L'Avenir d'Arcueil-Cachan)*, an American fashion magazine *(Vanity Fair)*, a mass circulation daily *(L'Humanité)*, and avant-garde reviews *(Le Cœur à Barbe, 391)*. When required, he even created his own medium, a newspaper entirely written and edited by himself *(Cartulaire)*; or turned the jottings in the margins of his own scores into graphically polished aphorisms.

Whether writing for the press, in a private letter, or advertising copy, he always gave his writing a personal twist. He would start a column such as *Memoirs of an Amnesic*, or *A Mammal's Notebooks*, and in opposition to the common practice of limiting a column to one paper, he would extend it, sometimes simultaneously, across several publications. Perhaps because he was concerned that he might lose contact with himself (he knew all too well that contact with him was not easy), he once posted a letter to himself to arrange a meeting for the morrow. And he carefully presented to himself his own day dreams, by writing them up in the style of small advertisements.

When it comes to his music, titles and

Erik Satie
Par lui-même

performance indications do not follow conventional practice either. They are dressed up as jokes in a Montmartre *chansonnier* vein (which many in the world of classical music found shocking), but for those that know how to decode them they provide the essential clues to the composition in question, or at least serve to underline its particular characteristics.

For instance, the title of *Three Pieces in the Form of a Pear*, on the one hand mocks the "*poires*" (which can be translated as "suckers") who cannot recognise a musical form which does not follow academic rules; and yet refers most of all to a spinning top, the "pear-shaped" toy which was very popular with children in Satie's day, and which went round and round eternally like the music of the *Three Pieces*.

The performance indications, which Satie insisted were strictly intended for the player and not the audience (one should not forget that in the days when Satie was composing, there was a piano in every household, and more or less everyone played a bit), were not aimed at the virtuoso wishing to display technique. They set out, rather, by the cumulative effect of seductive absurdities such as "on yellowing velvet," or "on the tips of your back teeth," to upset pianists' reasoning, undermine what they had been taught, and make them more open-minded and receptive to the message he wanted to put across.

Baron Medusa, the protagonist of Satie's only theatrical work, who doubles as a self-portrait of the composer, was expressing a similar outlook in claiming to belong to the "acephalous" class: that of headless creatures.

Satie never wrote an opera or a large symphonic work. His writings are rarely more than one page long, and usually take up only a few lines. "Keep it short" was the only advice he would give to his aspiring disciples, and his true model was the business letter: "You have something to say, and you say it." However, he carefully subtitled most of the texts he offered for publication as "fragments" or "extracts," as if they were drawn from a more extensive work to be found in another world. The fragments and extracts actually have a curious way of growing in the reader's mind. Jean Cocteau said appositely, "the smallest work by Satie is small in the way a keyhole is small. Everything changes when you put your eye to it." (or, one might add, your ear).

Satie's language, though majestic in his early writings, and mischievous in later years, remained constantly, throughout his life, both clear and simple, which does not exclude occasional rare words, frequently adding a twist to common expressions, or making unexpected combinations of terms one usually think of as incompatible.

In spite of a certain homogeneousness which makes them immediately recognisable, Satie's writings can be sorted according to their intended destination; whether they were addressed to his performers, to anyone and Everyone, or to himself alone; intended to be read (or not read) aloud, to be sung "as if being read," or merely acted.

Projet pour un buste de M. Erik SATIE (peint par lui-même), avec une pensée : « Je suis venu au monde très jeune dans un temps très vieux. »

No access of feeling or introspection is ever allowed to show in his writings, be they memoirs, poems, or pamphlets. Their principal subject is always the author's natural, or human surroundings — which never cease to cause him amazement. Most things were a source of wonder to him, the landscape, animals, children, and men — the latter obviously belonging to a species of which he did not see himself as a member.

A significant portion of his daydreams were given over to magical, minutely detailed descriptions of houses, manors and châteaux — which may have something to do with living for so long in a "cupboard," most of these ancient buildings being made of "cast iron." Debussy had described him as a "gentle medieval musician who had strayed into this century"; Satie was well aware that cast iron, as the quintessential building material of the industrial age, had been used to build the only tower he had seen erected in "this century" — the Eiffel Tower.

Satie always took a close interest in the visual arts; and worked with many of the greatest artists of his time — Picasso, Braque, Derain, Picabia; and most of all he examined their work very attentively. He even claimed that painters had "taught him much more about music than had composers." Man Ray called him the only musician "to have eyes"; in view of this it is no surprise that he should have devoted the meticulousness of a monkish scribe to the presentation of even the least important text or manuscript. He penned musical scores, articles, lecture notes, and private letters with the same stiff hand, with its carefully aligned upstrokes and down-strokes, sometimes enlivened with different coloured inks, which appears to aspire to the unchanging regularity of typographical characters.

The small ads he wrote purely for his own personal benefit were drawn without any crossings out, as if they came from a mould fully formed. They are like finely worked medallions, which one looks at with fascination before even thinking of reading what they say. His lecture notes, written in the humble school exercise books he was in the habit of using, are peppered strikingly with little strings of dots placed where he planned rhetorical pauses.

On some of his scores the arrangement of the notes on the stave succeeds in conveying visually the subject of the composition — for instance *Bathing* in the album *Sports & Recreations* imitates the waves on the sea. This is more than an innocent game. By exacerbating the graphic content, Satie prompts us to reflect on the paradox by which a composer is obliged to express himself in a form — graphic — which cannot be transmitted to a listener.

Etude pour un buste de M. Erik SATIE peinte par lui-même, avec une pensée: Je suis venu au monde très jeune dans un temps très vieux.

This volume sets out to present, with a brief commentary, an extensive selection from Erik Satie's varied non-musical output. The arrangement of the pieces is intended to help readers chart a course into the peculiar world of this "Mammal" who was the only member of his species.

Bon voyage!

Ornella Volta

TRANSLATOR'S NOTE

Satie knew what he had to say, and he said it. It was sometimes peculiar, frequently absurd, but that was always intended. A large amount of his writing is humorous, often consisting of extended deadpan passages which keep one wondering how much is literal, and how much ironic, until he reaches the final twist. He had a great love of puns and double entendres, which do not make life easy for the translator. I have attempted wherever possible to transfer this word-play into English. Of course there are cases where I had to back down and go with only one meaning, but where I have tried, I hope my attempts have not let him down; for Satie may be quizzical and odd, but he is rarely heavy-handed.

One major piece here is only Satie's by appropriation. I refer to *Socrates*, where I have translated into English Victor Cousin's translation into French of Plato's original Greek, as Satie carefully cut and collaged it. This may sound like Chinese whispers, and the French differs occasionally from modern English translations taken from the Greek, so it is worth saying that this book does not contain my translation of Plato, but of the French text that inspired Satie's finest musical work, and which he so lovingly transformed into a coherent and moving text; I have tried to preserve the timbre and rhythm of the French, as a text prepared for singing.

Translating Satie has provided moments of vexation, but never of dullness.

Antony Melville

1866

Eric Alfred Satie born on May 17th in Honfleur — where the Seine flows into the English Channel — of a Norman father and an English mother of Scottish ancestry.

Baptised into the Anglican church and taken on holiday to Brighton.

1872 After his mother's death his paternal grandparents have him re-baptised as a Catholic. First music lessons with the church organist, a graduate of the Niedermeyer school, keen on reviving Gregorian chant but also composer of slow waltzes.

1878 Admitted to the *Conservatoire de Musique et de Déclamation* in Paris; judged a "quite insignificant pupil."

1884 Composes his first piano work, *Allegro*, while on holiday in Honfleur. Spells his name with a 'k' — Erik — to stress his Viking ancestry.

1886 To get out of the *Conservatoire* he volunteers for the army, but then gets discharged after catching pneumonia — on purpose.

1887 Discovers the Chat Noir cabaret at the bottom of Montmartre, where free thinking and fantasy are the rule. Is nicknamed *Monsieur le Pauvre* — Satie insisted on remaining poor for the rest of his life.

1888 While Wagner and his "music of the future" are all the rage, Satie proposes to return to the "music of our origins" by composing three *Gymnopédies*.

1891 Meets Claude Debussy; the start of a long, close friendship, though not without its stormy patches.

1892 Named as "Chapel master to the Rose+Croix" by the Sâr Péladan, Grand Master of the order; he composes music for the Soirées de la Rose+Croix , which take place in the Symbolist painting Salon.

1893 Noisy break with the Rose + Croix, the better to refine "the independence of his aesthetic"; has a brief but intense affair with the painter Suzanne Valadon; then founds the Metropolitan Church of Art of Jesus Leader, of which he is the principal and sole adherent, to "combat society by means of music and painting." Composes the *Messe des Pauvres* for the ceremonies of his church which take place in the presence of himself alone, in the "cupboard" he lives in in Montmartre. His fellow Honfleurais Alphonse Allais nicknames him Esotérick Satie. Composes *Vexations*, a piece with 152 notes to be with played 840 times in succession, an important precursor of minimalism and repetitive music.

1896 Dumps his priestly robes overnight and buys seven identical velvet suits which he wears for the next seven years to the exclusion of all other clothes. He is now known as *The Velvet Gentleman.*

1898 Leaves Montmartre and goes to live in the suburbs south of Paris in a wretched room in the Maison des Quatre Cheminées in Arcueil-Cachan. Assiduous attendance at Café-concerts, where he earns his living as accompanist to Vincent Hyspa.

1903 Composes *Three Pieces in the Form of a Pear*, a sort of retrospective of his musical ideas from the last ten years.

1904 Composes *La Diva de l'Empire*, an "American intermezzo" for Paulette Darty, the "queen of the slow waltz."

1905 At the age of nearly forty, returns to school to study at the Schola Cantorum — counterpoint with Albert Roussel, and orchestration with Vincent d'Indy. He dresses in bureaucratic uniform, with a bowler hat, stiff collar, and umbrella.

1910 Retired to Arcueil, takes local schoolchildren on class expeditions, for which he is awarded the local "palmes académiques." Maurice Ravel, already famous, unexpectedly "rediscovers" him as a precursor of Debussy and himself, and brings him back to the heart of Parisian musical life. Meets Igor Stravinsky.

1912 Supported by young composers and writers around the *Revue Musicale S.I.M.*, for which he begins writing his *Memoirs of an Amnesic*. Teams up with the great pianist Ricardo Viñes and writes fifty or so "fantasy" pieces for him, of which the central item is the musical album *Sports & Recreations*, written to drawings by Charles Martin.

1917 Meets Jean Cocteau, Pablo Picasso and Serge Diaghilev, and composes with them, in the middle of the First World War, the ballet *Parade*, which is a resounding *succès de scandale.*

1918 Composes his "symphonic drama," *Socrates*, to Plato's *Dialogues*, for one of the receptions given by Princess Edmond de Polignac. Brancusi makes sculptures inspired by it.

1920 The *Groupe des Six* is formed under his banner. He presents in an art gallery his first piece of *Musique d'Ameublement* (Furniture Music) "Music not to be listened to," now seen as one of the beginnings of Ambient music.

1921 His "lyrical comedy," *Medusa's Snare*, written in 1913, is staged at the Théâtre Michel and published by D.H. Kahnweiler, the cubist art dealer, with engravings by Georges Braque.

1922 An active member of Montparnasse literary and artistic circles; he contributes to avant-garde reviews and is a friend of André Derain, Brancusi, Tristan Tzara, Marcel Duchamp, Man Ray. Is on bad terms with André Breton and the future Surrealists.

ERIK SATIE

COMPOSITEUR DE MUSIQUE D'AMEUBLEMENT

Musicien de la Confrérie de la Rose + Croix

MAITRE DE CHAPELLE DE L'ÉGLISE MÉTROPOLITAINE DE JÉSUS CONDUCTEUR ÉLÈVE DIPLOMÉ DE LA SCHOLA CANTORUM

➤ — VOUS PRÉSENTE — →

1923 The *Ecole d'Arcueil* is formed under his banner.

1924 Composes the ballet *Mercure*, with "plastic poses" by Pablo Picasso, for Comte Etienne de Beaumont's soirées, and the "instantaneist" ballet *Relâche*, with script, sets, and costumes by Francis Picabia. For the interval he composes the first "frame by frame" film music — some years before the movies stopped being silent.

1925 1st July. Satie dies in the Hôpital Saint Joseph, from cyrrhosis of the liver complicated by pleurisy. His room in Arcueil, to which no one had been admitted while he was alive, reveals, amid extraordinary pandemonium, precious unpublished manuscripts and thousands of tiny papers with calligraphic inscriptions describing a "looking glass" world.

I. WRITTEN FOR PERFORMANCE

To Whom It May Concern[1]

    I forbid reading the text aloud in the course of musical performance. Any failure to observe this requirement will incur my righteous indignation against the presuming party.

    No special cases will be allowed.

Erik Satie

AUTOMATIC DESCRIPTIONS[2]

1. On a Vessel

At the mercy of the breakers.
Splash of spray;
Another;
Fresh puff of wind.
Maritime melancholy.
Splash of spray;
Gentle pitching once again;
Little wave.
The captain says: Very nice
    crossing.
The vessel grins.
Landscape in the distance;
Little breeze;
Polite little splash of spray;
To bring us in to shore.

2. On a Lantern

Do not light up yet: you have
    plenty of time.
You can light up now, if you like.
Shine a little in front of you;
Your hand in front of the light;
Take your hand away and put it
    in your pocket.
Ssh! Wait.
Put it out.

3. On a Helmet

They are coming.
What a lot of people!
It is magnificent!
Here are the drums!
That is the colonel, that fine man
    walking alone,
Heavy as a sow,
Light as an egg.

DRIED EMBRYOS[3]

1. Of Holothuria

Vulgarly known as "sea cucumber." Holothuria generally climbs on stones or pieces of rock. Like the cat, this animal purrs; it also spins a revolting kind of silk. The action of light seems to upset it. I observed an Holothuria in Saint-Malo bay.

Out in the morning. It is raining.
The sun is in the clouds.
Little purr. What a pretty rock!
It is nice to be alive.
Like a nightingale with
    toothache.
Back home in the evening. It is
    raining.
The sun is not there any more.

As long as it never comes back.
Mocking little purr.
It was a really good rock. Nice
    and sticky.
Don't make me laugh, bit of
    foam: you are tickling me.
I haven't any tobacco.
Lucky I don't smoke.

2. Of Edriophthalma

Crustaceans with sessile eyes, that is to say, stalkless and immobile. Being naturally very sad, these crustaceans live in seclusion from the world, in holes pierced through the cliffs.

They are all together.
Oh how sad!
A responsible father starts to
    speak.
They all start weeping.
Poor creatures!
How well he spoke.
Big groan.

3. Of Podophthalma

Crustaceans with their eyes on the end of moving stalks. They are nimble, indefatigable hunters. They are to be found in every sea. The flesh of Podophthalma is tasty and nourishing.

Out hunting. The chase.
An advisor. He is right!
To cast a spell on the quarry.
What is it?
The advisor.

18

CHAPTERS TURNED THIS WAY AND THAT[4]

1. She Who Talks Too Much

Let me speak. Listen to me.
Interior with respectable people.
The beauties of existence and
    department stores.
The wife explains to her husband:
I want a solid mahogany hat.
Mrs. Thing had an umbrella
    completely made of bone.
Let me speak.
Miss What's-it is marrying a
    man who is as dry as a cuckoo.
Let me.
Just listen to me.
He dies of exhaustion.

2. The Man Who Carries Big Stones

He carries them on his back. He smirks and looks very sure of himself. His strength amazes the little children. We see him transporting an enormous rock, a hundred times bigger than himself (it is a pumice stone).

Straining.
Painfully and jerkily.
Dragging his feet.
He can feel he is losing hold of
    the stone: it is going to fall.
That is it: *it falls off.*

3. The Prisoners' Lament (Jonah and Latude)

They are doing time.
They meditate.
They are several centuries apart.
Jonah says: I am a sea-going
    Latude.
Latude says: I am a French Jonah.
It smells shut in, they think.
They imagine they can see the
    good old sun.
They think only of getting out.

19

OLD SEQUINS & OLD BREAST PLATES[5]

1. At the Gold-Merchant's (Venice, XIIIth Century)

He strokes his gold
He covers it in kisses.
He hugs an old bag.
He puts ten thousand gold francs
    in his mouth.
He picks up a piece of gold and
    talks to it softly.
He prances around.
He is happy as a king.
He rolls in a coffer with his head
    down.
He comes out all stooping and
    stiff.

2. Dance in Armour (Greek Period)

This is danced in two rows.
The first row do not move.
The second row stand still.
Each of the dancers is hit with a
    sabre which splits his head
    open.

3. Defeat of the Cimbrians (Nightmare)

A tiny child is asleep in his tiny bed. His very aged grandfather gives him every day an odd little sort of course in general history, dredged up from his vague memories. Often he talks about the famous King Dagobert, about Monsieur the Duke of Marlborough, and the great Roman general Marius. In his dreams, the tiny child sees these heroes fighting the Cimbrians, on the field of Mons-en-Puelle (1304).

Rain of javelins.
Portrait of Marius.
Boïorix, King of the Cimbrians.
He is full of sorrow.
Villars' dragoons.
The coronation of Charles X.

[THREE NEW CHILDREN'S PIECES][6]

Nasty Little Good-for-nothing

His mother ticks him off.
He has the cheek to laugh.
She tells him he is naughty.
He has the cheek to laugh.
She tells him he shall have no
    more jam.
He has the cheek to laugh; he is
    incorrigible.

The Sweet Little Tiny Girl

She is very good
She loves her doll.
She talks to it softly.
What a sweet little girl!
Which is why her doll loves her
    very much,
What big eyes the doll has got!
It is because she would like to
    speak.

KO-QUO'S CHILDHOOD[7]

(Motherly advice)

*1. Do not drink your chocolate with
    your fingers*

Wait for it to cool down a bit
Well! You've burnt your tongue
— No, Mummy: I've swallowed
    the spoon.

2. Do not blow in your ears

You are unbearable
Do not tread on my feet
You would try the patience of a
    horse.

*3. Do not put your head under your
    arm*

If you get in the habit of behaving
nicely, you might end up as a
Field-Marshal. And who knows?
Your head might be blown off by
a cannon-ball. Which is a fine
thing for a boy! You would be an
old soldier with a wooden head.

CHILDISH PRATTLE[8]

1. The King of the Beans' War Song

What a merry King!
His face is all red.
He knows how to dance, in his
    own right.
His nose is covered in hairs.
He slaps his belly.
When he laughs, he's at it for an
    hour or more.
What a good King!
He is a great warrior.
You should see him on a horse.
He wears a red hat.
His horse knows how to dance, in
    its own right.
He gives his horse big whacks.
It is a good horse.
It even likes war and cannon-
    balls.
What a fine horse!

2. What the Tulip Princess Said

I like cabbage soup very much,
    but I like my little Mummy
    even more.
Can we speak quietly? My doll
    has got a headache.
She fell down from the 3rd floor.
The doctor says it is nothing.

3. The Almond Chocolate Waltz

You shall have a bit.
Do you like chocolate? Let it
    melt in your mouth.
Mummy, there is a bone in it.
No, my love, it is an almond.
The little boy wants to eat the
    whole box.
My, he is greedy!
His mummy gently tells him not
    to: he must not make himself
    sick.
How dreadful! he is stamping
    with rage.

COLOURFUL CHILDISH PURSUITS[9]

1. Little Prelude to the Day

Get up nicely.
Stand up nicely.
Brush your hair nicely.
Look at yourself nicely.
Behave yourself nicely.
Go for a walk nicely.
Look after yourself nicely.

2. Lullaby

The day is done, and Pierrot is
    going to bed.
He has been very, very good.
His mother gives him a kiss.
He gets into bed feeling pleased
    with himself, and says:
"Will Grandpa and Grandma
    know that I have been very
    good?"
Yes, Mummy answers.
"Who will tell them?"
"They will see it in the paper."
Pierrot goes to sleep, proud as
    can be.

3. Steps of the Grand Staircase

It is a grand staircase, very grand.
It has more than a thousand
    steps, all made of ivory.
It is very beautiful.
No one dares to use it for fear of
    spoiling it.
The King himself has never used
    it.
To leave his room, he jumps out
    of the window.
And often he says:
"I love this staircase so much I
    am going to have it stuffed."
The King is right, isn't he?

TIRESOME PECCADILLOES[10]

1. Being Jealous of your Friend Who Has Got a Big Head.

A jealous person is not a happy
    person.
I once knew a boy who was
    jealous of his parrot.
He wanted to know his lessons as
    well as the parrot knew his.

2. Eating his Bread and Butter

Get used to seeing bread and
    butter without feeling the need
    to pinch it.
It could make your head swell up
    if you touch a friend's bread
    and butter.
I had a dog once who secretly
    smoked all my cigars.
It made him ill in his tummy.
And that upset his Daddy
    terribly!

3. Taking Advantage of the Fact he has Corns on his Feet to Pinch his Hoop

You just do not do that.
If the Good Lord sees, he will be
    furious.
It is something you should never
    do, unless you are told to.

BOTHERSOME GLOBS[11]

1. The Look in her Eyes

Her look is a tepid adornment.
You can see it when she opens her
    eyes.
What is it seeking?
The beauty of ships that ride the
    waves?
The old nightingale's hiding-
    place?
The house where the poet was
    born?
No: she is about to go out &
    cannot find her pig-silk sun-
    shade, the one that looks like a
    tomato.

2. Piping

What is that lovely thread of
    water running through this
    soft land?
It is so shy.
It hides under the ground.
Is it a smile from the landscape?
Is it an anonymous gift of
    Nature?
Is it an exquisite tear, wrung
    from the rocks?
I do not think so: it is the main
    sewer.

INSIPID MEMORIES[12]

Scrawl

The old house which squats at the edge of the wood is badly painted,
    badly drawn & above all very uncomfortable. It houses some rakes, a
    few shovels, some watering-cans and an old gardener.
Our landscape painters refuse to portray the features of the old house,
    with its rakes, & shovels & watering-cans & the old gardener.
It is just a lot of scrawl.

Hair

The hare has lost its hair: the one it had on its nose.
His friends used to call him "Hairy" to distinguish him from other hares.
From now on he will be called "Smoothy," a less glorious designation.
His fiancée will not want anything more to do with him, his future
    children will be diminished by this, his co-religionaries (those who
    practise the same religion as him) will turn away on seeing him.
Here we see him weeping at his misfortune, though he has dry eyes and
    a smile upon his lips.

REVERIE ON A DISH[13]

How white it is!
No paint adorns it.
It is one single piece.

SPORTS & RECREATIONS[14]

Previously unpublished drawings by Charles Martin, 1914.

Unappetising Chorale

Grim and cantankerous.

The Swing

It is my heart that swings so.
It is not dizzy.
It has such tiny feet.
Will it ever come back inside my
    chest?

Hunting

Can you hear the rabbit singing?
What a voice!
The owl is suckling its young.
The nightingale is in its burrow.
The boar is getting married.
And I am shooting nuts down
    with my gun.

26

Italian Comedy

Scaramouche explains the
  beauties of military life.
It makes you very smart, he says.
You frighten civilians.
And adventures with the ladies!
  and all!
What a lovely job!

The Bride's Reveille

The procession arrives.
Guitars made of old hats.
Stand up everyone!
A dog is dancing with his fiancée.

Blind Man's Buff

Look hard, Mademoiselle.
The one who loves you is a step
    away.
How pale he is; his lips tremble.
    You laugh?
He holds his heart in both hands.
But you pass by without
    guessing.

Fishing

The lapping of water in a river-
    bed.
A fish comes, then another, then
    two more.
"What is it?"
"It is a fisherman, a poor
    fisherman."
"Thank you."
Everyone goes home, including
    the fisherman.
The lapping of water in a river-
    bed.

Yachting

What weather! The wind is
    puffing and blowing like a seal.
The yacht dances.
It looks like a little madman.
The sea has been taken apart.
As long as it does not break up on
    a rock.
No one can put it together again.
"I do not wish to stay here," says
    the pretty passenger.
"It is not an amusing spot.
I would prefer something else.
Go and fetch me a carriage."

Bathing

The sea is wide, Madame.
In any case, it is pretty deep.
Do not sit on the bottom.
It is very damp.
Here come some nice old waves.
They are full of water.
You are completely soaked!
"Yes, I am, Sir."

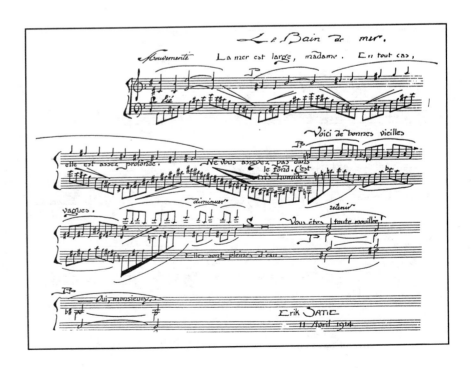

Carnival

The confetti pours down!
Here is a melancholy mask.
A Pierrot is being clever.
Some flowing cloaks arrive.
People push to see.
"Are they pretty?"

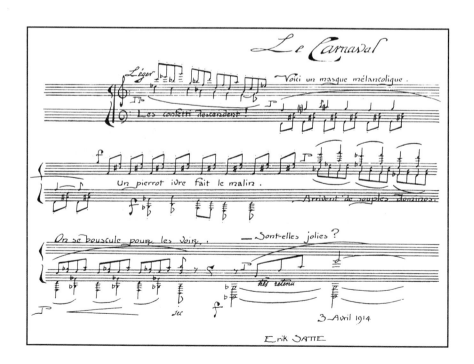

Golf

The colonel is wearing shocking
    green "Scotch Tweed."
He will be victorious.
His "caddie" follows him,
    carrying his "bags."
The clouds are amazed.
The "holes" are all a-tremble: the
    colonel is here!
And now he is playing his shot:
His "club" flies into pieces!

The Octopus

The octopus is in her cave.
She is playing with a crab.
She chases it.
She has swallowed it sideways on.
Her face turns haggard, she trips
    over her feet.
She drinks a glass of salt water to
    make herself feel better.
The drink does her a lot of good
    and takes her mind off it.

The Races

Weighing in. Buying the
    programme. Twenty each way.
On the starting line. They are off.
Punters lying low.
The losers (noses pointed and
    ears down).

Puss in the Corner

The four mice. The cat.
The mice annoy the cat.
The cat rises up.
It springs.
The cat is in the corner.

The Picnic

They have all brought very cold
   veal.
"You have a lovely white dress."
"Listen, an aeroplane."
"Oh no, it is a storm."

The Water-chute

"If you have a strong stomach,
   you will not be too ill.
You will feel as if you are falling
   off the scaffolding.
It is very curious, you will see.
Careful, now! Do not change
   colour."
"I feel ill at ease."
"That shows you need some fun."

Non-stop Tango

The Tango is the Devil's dance.
It is his favourite.
He dances it to cool down.
His wife, his daughters and his
    servants cool themselves down
    that way.

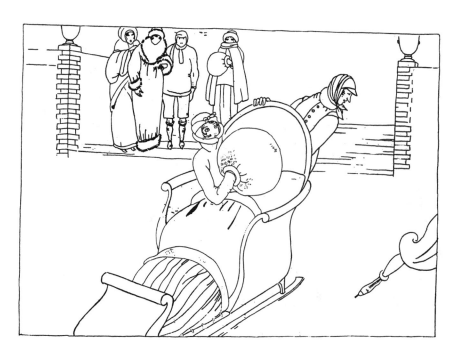

The Sledge

My, it is cold!
"Ladies, put your noses down in
    your furs."
The sledge is off.
The landscape is very cold and
    does not know where to put
    itself.

Flirting

They say pretty things to each
    other, modern things.
"How are you?"
"Aren't I nice?"
"Leave me alone."
"You have big eyes."
"I would like to be on the moon."
He sighs.
He nods his head.

Fireworks

It is so dark! Oh, a Bengal Light!
A rocket, a bright blue rocket.
Everyone thinks it is wonderful.
An old man goes mad.
The Grand Finale.

Tennis

Shall we play? Yes. Good serve.
What lovely legs he has!
He has a handsome nose.
Service out.
Game!

INSTANTANEOUS CENTURIES-OLD HOURS[15]

To Sir William Grant-Plumot I genially dedicate this group of pieces. Two figures have surprised me up to now: Louis XI and Sir William. The first by his strange form of good naturedness; the second, by his continuous immobility. I am honoured to pronounce here the names of Louis XI and Sir William Grant-Plumot.

Erik Satie

1. Venomous Obstacles

This vast part of the world is inhabited by one single man: a negro.
He is so bored he could die of laughing.
It is 9.17 by the shadow of the thousand-year-old trees.
The toads call each other by their proper name.
To help him think, the negro holds his cerebellum in his right hand with the fingers apart.
From afar, he looks like a distinguished physiologist.
Four anonymous serpents enthral him, hanging suspended from the coat tails of his uniform which is
     distorted with a combination of grief and loneliness.
On the banks of the river an aged mangrove slowly washes its revoltingly dirty roots.
It is not the trysting hour.

2. Morning Twilight (At Midday)

The sun has got up nice and early and in a good mood.
The heat will be greater than normal, for the weather is prehistoric and set for a storm.
The sun is right at the top of the sky; he looks like a nice chap.
But don't let us trust him.
He may be going to burn the crops, or strike us terribly: with sun-stroke.
Behind the barn, an ox is eating itself sick.

3. Haywire in Granite

The clock in the old deserted village is also going to strike most terribly: to strike thirteen.
Antediluvian rain comes down from the clouds of dust. The great grinning woods are stretching out their branches;
     while rough granite boulders jostle and do not know where to put themselves so as to get in the way.
Thirteen is about to strike in the guise of one in the afternoon.
Alas! the clocks have not gone back.

41

THREE ELEGANT WALTZES BY A SQUEAMISH PANSY[16]

1. His Waist

Those that harm the reputation or the wealth of others rather than forgo a witticism, deserve degrading punishment. This needed to be said, and I am prepared to say it.

    LA BRUYÈRE, *Les Caractères ou Les Moeurs de ce siècle*, in the edition by MM. G. Servois and A. Rebelliau.

He looks at himself.
He hums a XVth century air.
Then, he pays himself a nicely-
    fitting compliment.
Who will dare to say he is not the
    most handsome?
His heart is tender, is it not?
He puts his arm around his waist.
He finds it quite ravishing.
What will the pretty marchioness
    say?
She will struggle, but be
    overcome.
Yes, Madam.
Is it not written thus?

2. His Pince-Nez

Our ancient custom forbade pubescent youths to show themselves naked in the baths, and modesty thus took deep root in our souls.

    CICERO, *de re publica.*

He cleans them every day.
They are silver-rimmed pince-nez
    with smoked gold lenses.
They were given him by a
    beautiful Lady. Such fine
    memories!
But... great sorrow comes over
    our friend: he has lost the case
    for these pince-nez.

3. His Legs

The owner's first concern when he arrives at his farm should be to greet his household Penates; then the same day, if he has time, he should walk round his property; he should see what state his crops are in; what work has been done, and what has not.

    CATO, *de rustica.*

He is very proud of them.
They dance only the choicest
    dances.
They are nice flat legs.
In the evening they are dressed in
    black.
He wants to carry them under his
    arm.
They slide along melancholically.
And now they are indignant, very
    angry.
Often he kisses them, and puts
    them round his neck.
He is so good to them!
He refuses categorically to buy
    gaiters.
"A prison," he says.

THOUGHTS-BEFORE-LAST[17]

1. Idyll

What do I see? The Stream is all wet; and the Woods are inflammable and dry as garden rakes.
But my heart is ever so small.
The Trees are like big badly made combs; and the Sun has nice gold rays piled up like a beehive.
But my heart has a shiver in its spine.
The Moon has quarrelled with its neighbours; and the Stream is soaked to the skin.

2. Aubade

Do not sleep, sleeping beauty.
Listen to the voice of your True-love.
He skips a rigadoon. He loves you so.
He is a poet.
Can you hear him? Is he just sniggering?
No; he adores you, sweet Beauty!
He skips another rigadoon and catches a cold.
Don't you want to love him?
He is a poet, though, an old poet!

3. Meditation

The poet is shut up in his old tower.
Here comes the wind.
The poet meditates, without appearing to.
All of a sudden he gets goose-flesh.
Why?
Here is the Devil! No, not him: it is the wind, the wind of genius passing.
The Poet has his head full, of wind!
He smiles mischievously, while his heart is weeping like a willow.
But Genius is there watching him with an evil eye: a glass eye.
And the Poet goes all humble and all red.
He cannot meditate any more:
He has indigestion!
Terrible indigestion all maggoty with blank verse and bitter Disillusionment!

BUREAUCRATIC SONATINA[18]

Allegro

He's leaving home.
He goes gaily off to his office, gavilling as he goes.
He nods his head contentedly.
He loves a very elegant young lady.
He also loves his pen-holder,
    his shiny green over-sleeves,
    and his Chinese skull-cap.
He takes big strides.
He rushes up the staircase and climbs it on his back.
What a gust of wind!
Sitting in his chair, he is happy and he shows it.

Andante

He thinks about his prospects for promotion.
Maybe he will get a pay rise without needing
    promotion.
He is planning to move when his lease comes due.
There is a flat he has his eye on.
He really must have a promotion or a pay rise!
Further thoughts about promotion.

Vivache

He hums an old Peruvian air
which he collected from a deaf-mute in Lower
    Brittany.
A neighbouring piano is playing Clementi.
It is so sad!
He dares to dance (he does, not the piano).
This is really all very sad.
The piano starts work again.
Our friend questions himself gently.
The cool Peruvian air goes to his head again.
The piano goes on.
Alas! he must leave his office, his lovely office.
"Come on, now," he says, "Let's go."

FAKE NOCTURNE[19]

The night is silent.
The melancholy is huge.
A will-o-'the-wisp troubles the tranquil landscape.
What a bore! It is an old-will-o'-the-wisp.
Did it really have to come?
Let's go back to our dreaming, please.

[**TRILOGY**][20]

1. Paul & Virginie

Virginie sang like a gorgeous little potato.
Virginie's singing made the monkeys weep.
So Paul danced on one foot so as not to bother his parents.
Virginie liked watching him dance.

2. Robinson Crusoe

In the evening they ate their soup, & went to smoke their pipes beside the sea.
The smell of tobacco made the fishes sneeze.
Robinson Crusoe did not find it much fun on his desert island.
"It is really too deserted," he said.
His negro Friday agreed. He said to his good master:
"Yes, Mistah; a desert island is really too deserted."
And he nodded his big black head.

PERFORMANCE INDICATIONS[21]

A bit hot
A bit rococo but slow
Advise yourself most carefully
A little cooked
A little warm
Alone, for a moment
Alone, opposite
A lot of expression and slower
Almost invisible
Apply within yourself
Apply yourself to renunciation
Arching your back
As if you were congested
As quiet as Baptiste
Assertively
Attaching too much importance
Attentively
At the top of your voice, don't
    you think?
Avoid any sacrilegious
    excitement

Be an hour late
Be-dig yourself
Be fixed
Behave yourself, please: a monkey
    is watching you
Behind
Be invited
Be unaware of your own presence
Be visible for a moment
Blackish
Both hands together
Bounce back scantily
Breathe
Broad as possible
Broadening your head

Broaden your impression
Brutal
Bury the sound

Caeremoniosus
Calm and profoundly gentle
Calm without slowness
Carefully
Caressing
Carried away
Carry that further
Casually
Cautiously and slowly
Cloisterly
Coldly
Continue without losing
consciousness
Convince
Corpulentus

Courageously easy and obligingly
    alone
Cultivate renunciation
Cumulatively
Curtain

Dance inwardly
Dancing
Deferentially
Detached but not dry
Determined
Do as I do
Do not change your physiognomy
Do not come out of your shadow
Do not cough
Do not eat too much
Do not go out
Do not inflate
Do not look disagreeable
Do not lose your bearings
Do not speak

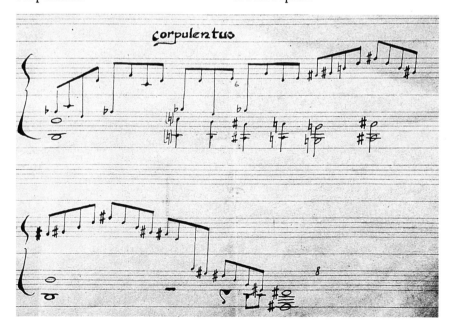

Do not swallow
Do not sweat
Do not torment yourself
Dry as a cuckoo

End for yourself
Energetic
Energetically
Enigmatic
Enthusiastically
Epotus
Even duller if you can
Even whiter if possible

Fairly alert
Fall till you are weak
Fascinatedly
Fast
Fatten
Fidgety
Fierce and forbidding
Flat on the floor
Floating
Fold carefully
Fold gently
From a distance, bored
From afar
From the top of yourself
Full of subtlety, if you believe me

Gaily
Gawp
Gently
Genuinely
Get late bit by bit without equi-
      vocation
Get soaked
Gird yourself with perceptiveness
Give orders quietly

Go away!
Go down
Go on
Good-naturedly
Graciously
Grandiose
Grandly forgetting the present
Grow bigger
Grow pale
Gummy

Haggard in your body
Half way
Hard as the devil?
Have a drink
Heavy
High
Hold back
Hypocritically

Illusorius
Imbibe

Comme un rossignol qui aurait mal aux dents

Imitativus
Impassive
Important
In a very peculiar manner
Indubitable
Inevitably
Inflexible
In force

In one breath
In the back of your throat
In the best
In the deepest silence
In the pit of your belly
In the ribs
Into the slow
In your head
Ironically
Is your feeling mellow?

Lacquered like a chinaman
Lastly
Laugh without anyone knowing
Learnedly
Light as an egg
Light, but decent
Light, but loud
Lightly animated
Lights out
Like a beast
Like a gentle request

Like a nightingale with toothache
Look closely, that is all
Looking at yourself from afar
Looking at it twice
Look like a fraud

Meanly
Melancholy

Moderate and very bored
Moderate joy
Modestly
More intimately
More relaxedly
Mysterious and tender

Naturally
Neapolitan
Necessarily
Nice
Nobly
Nocturnally

Obligingly
One step at a time
On fire
On the tip of your mind
On the tips of your back teeth
On yellowing velvet
On your tongue
Opacus
Open your head
Out of the corner of your hand
Outward, painfully

Paedagogus

Play out, don't you think?
Play right out
Pleasurably, without shyness
Plenty of action
Positively
Preciously
Push apart
Put yourself in the shade

Questioning
Quite blue
Quite slow
Quite well done
Quiver like a leaf

Rather cold
Rather slow, if you would
Riddled
Rise on your fingers
Rising
Rocking
Run

Sad
Sad and more and more calm
Same assertiveness but more
    inward
Scratch
Second helping
Seriously but without tears
Shake yourself
Silently, please
Sing
Sing seriously
Skilfully
Slow and grave
Slow and painful
Slow down good-naturedly
Slow down kindly

Nocturnus
Noiselessly, believe me again.
Not too rare

Obey

Pale and priest-like
Paululum
Peacefully
Perfect
Physiognomical

Slow down mentally
Slow down politely
Smile
So as to make a hollow
Sombre
Sound surprised
Stay (half a second) right in front
    of you
Steady as she goes
Sticky
Stir it up inside
Straight in front of you
Subitus
Substantialis
Superstitiously
Supple

Take your hand off and put it in
    your pocket
Tell yourself about it
Tender
Tough as the devil
Try some more
Turbulent
Turn pale

Under the pomegranates
Up on your fingers

Very affectionate
Very boring
Very carefully
Very Christian
Very down to earth
Very far away
Very lost
Very much
Very nice
Very sheepish

Very shining
Very sincerely silent
Very sticky
Very suitable
Very Turkish
Very white
Virtuous
Visible for a moment

Weep like a willow
Weighty
White
White and immobile
Whiter
Wholly and completely
Winking
With a broad view
With a full chest
With a healthy superiority
With amazement
With both hands
With camaraderie
With ceremony
With conviction and stern
    sadness
With delicate intimacy
With great goodness
With great seriousness and
    courteous gravity
With inane but appropriate
    naivety
Without batting an eyelid too
    much
Without getting annoyed
Without grandeur
Without hurrying
Without ostentation
Without pride
Without trembling too much

Without wickedness
Without your fingers blushing
With righteous anger
With sadness
With sadness and inevitability
With shy piety
With slowness
With tears in your fingers
With tenderness
With the flow
With the tips of your eyes and
    holding back in advance
With timid piety
With your body
With your bones dry and distant
With your hand above
With your hand on your
    conscience
With your head between your
    hands
With no shine

You see

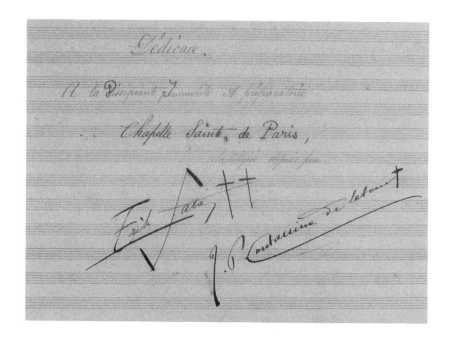

uspud[22]

Christian ballet in three acts by J.P.Contamine de Latour
Sacred music in three acts by Erik Satie

True genealogical development from which Uspud descends.
Irnebizolle, Uspud's sister; Jindebude, mother of Saint Plan; Ytunube, son of Corcleru; Uspud, son of Saint Plan; Ontrotance, cousin of Saint Benu; Saint Plan, brother of Tumisrudebude; Corcleru, uncle of Apufonse; Saint Induciomare, brother of Yturrube; Saint Micanar, cousin of Entimedu; Gulbejare, brother of Irnebizolle; Apufonse, brother of Ontrotance; Saint Benu, sister of Jindebude; Entimedu, uncle of Saint Cleophemus, Saint Marcomir, father of Saint Benu; Saint Cleophemus, great uncle of Uspud; Tumisrudebude, mother of Gulbejare.

Paris, 17th of the month of November of 1892

Dedication
To the most August, Permanent, and Luminous Indivisibility of the Three Persons of the Holy Trinity.

J.P.Contamine de Latour † Erik Satie ††
Paris, 17th of the month of Novemberof 1892

Sole character:
USPUD, young, very rich pagan; a handsome young man greatly valued in ancient society.

Spiritual characters:
Our Holy Mother the Church, Jesus on the Cross, Cherubim, Virgins, Thrones, Powers, Dominions, etc; invisible Wings; flaming Hair; Constellations; diverse Trees and a variety of Animals; Phenomena and natural elements.

One or two testimonials

to the goodness, usefulness, and shining truth contained in this work, emanating from the spirits of several competent inhabitants of the other world (three hermetic wizards were turning the tables):

Karl Linnaeus, naturalist

François de Solignac, de la Mothe de Fénelon, ecclesiastic (took great pleasure from the end of Act Two)

Mehemet Ali, General at the head of an army

Jean-Paul Marat, deputy (Marat's opinion of this work is merely optional)

Louise de Savoie, woman from Orleans, of no profession

William Shakspeare (sic), playwright

Longus, man of letters

Lycurgus, advocate

François Machiavel, publicist (has not yet heard Act One; very much liked the other two)

Eustache Lesueur, painter

Michel Le Cellier, Marquis de Louvois, former minister

Gutenberg, printer (particularly liked the middle of Act One)

Caius Marius, Brigadier-General

Samuel, Isaac, Abel, Nathan, Mathias, Aron Levy, Professor of Catholic theology

Rameau, composer of music (thinks it will be a great success)

Guy Patin, Doctor of Medicine

Michel de Montaigne, philosopher

The Emperor Julian the Apostate, head of State

Thomas More, diplomat

Jacques Necker, banker, former minister

These highly valued testimonials were obtained with the use of extraordinarily heavy tables.

Erik Satie †† J.P.Contamine de Latour †

ACT ONE

A desert.

Statues, on enormous pedestals, are arranged in a semi-circle. In the middle, a table with the remains of a feast. To one side, a barrel, bristling with nails inside; in the distance corpses and human bones.

USPUD appears at the back of the desert, playing knuckle-bones with some shin-bones; he crushes the shin-bones, puts the powder into an incense burner, and sprinkles each of the statues.

The smoke from it changes into Cherub's wings which flutter in the air.

USPUD collapses.

He hides his face in his hands and sinks deep in thought.

Young girls dressed in white and bearing sistra gambol in the air.

Suddenly the air turns white. A woman of great beauty, transparent as crystal, appears before USPUD. It is the Christian Church; she throws aside her dark mantle and stands clad in a golden tunic.

USPUD in surprise takes some sand and rubs his eyes.

Then he throws stones at the apparition. The stones become balls of fire which burst noisily; the last and biggest lets out flames.

At the same time a great thunder-clap is heard: the statues collapse, grinding their teeth.

A volcano rises where the dining table stood, and the crater spits out stars.

USPUD falls unconscious.

When he revives, his beard has grown and his hair has turned white.

End of Act One

ACT TWO

Same decor.

USPUD in a yellow robe and astrakhan hat. USPUD reflects profoundly upon paganism. He wants to worship statues, but they change, and in succession bear the heads of animals: dog, then jackal, tortoise, goat, fish, lynx, tiger, wolf, ox, sea-woodcock, unicorn, sheep, antelope, ant, spider, gnu, snake, agouti, blue goat, baboon, cuckooloo, crab, albatross, pacre, ostrich, mole, secretary-bird, old bull, red caterpillar, bonti, pagos, wild boar, crocodile and buffalo.

USPUD wants to bury himself but is surrounded by a ring of black bitches, with golden horns on their foreheads, which bark and shake themselves as they walk round and round him.

USPUD is afraid and tries to kill himself by jumping into the barrel: the barrel bursts and comes back together as soon as he has gone. He offers a prayer to the statues of the gods, who now take the shape of trees and plants: myrrh, lotus, rubber tree, cedar, coconut palm, aloe, palm-tree, oak, spindle &c.

Rain falls; stinking lakes appear on the ground, and the emanations bubbling from them form monstrous frogs which flutter in the air. Far off the flames of a burning house can be descried.

A vast storm is unleashed; mountains of petrified sand rise up, chasms yawn, caves are hollowed out. The statues fall with a noise from hell. USPUD, crushed, calls upon heaven for help.

Now the Christian Church appears, and the bitches run off howling: amid the lightning, crucifixes fly through space, and in the air USPUD sees a vision of a pagan court of justice — arrows, chopping blocks, racks, hatchets, red-hot irons, and every instrument of torture, covered in blood.

It rains blood, severed heads, and shreds of burnt flesh, for a very long time.

The Christian Church grows inordinately large, and becomes more transparent; as she fades she stretches out her arms to USPUD and an intense clarity takes the place of the fog and the visions.

A huge Christ comes out of the earth and rises to heaven, at the same time as the Church. When they are gone, choirs can be heard of angels, archangels, cherubim, Powers, Thrones and Dominions, and the Blessed, singing their hymn.

Slowly the clarity fades, and normal daylight returns. USPUD, alone amid the debris of statues and crockery, raises his arms to heaven with an ecstatic smile;

then he falls with his face to the ground, tears his yellow robe, under which can be seen a camel's-hair tabard. He tears out his beard, and cries out with all his might: I am a Christian!

End of Act Two.

54

ACT THREE

Same decor without the props — except the barrel.

USPUD lies prostrate before a crucifix. For a long time he remains without moving.

Suddenly he gets up, lets down his hair, tears the bottom of his robe and plunges the piece of cloth deep into the barrel; he pulls it out soaked in water which he runs over his forehead, saying:

"I baptise myself in the name of the Father, the Son and the Holy Ghost." His robe turns green.

Christ rises into the air. USPUD stretches his arms towards him.

Then a great faith passes through him: a mystical radiance shines from his face — he knows both truth and happiness; he dances and claps his hands; flaming locks of hair twirl around him.

He stops, feeling an inextinguishable thirst for suffering.

A long line of martyred saints parades before him, in the heavens.

Saint Cleophemus spits his teeth into his hand.

Saint Micanar tears out his cheeks; the blessed Marcomir carries his head under his arm; Saint Induciomare plunges arrows into his legs.

Once the procession has gone, USPUD hears voices calling him to martyrdom; he glimpses palms and crowns; and so, caught in a frenzy of suffering, he swallows sand, cuts off his eyelids with sharp stones and lacerates his body.

He suffers and is happy.

Restless dance.

USPUD wants to die, creeps into the barrel among the nails, and rolls around inside. He comes out horribly swollen and wishes he were no longer alive.

A black bitch, with a sort of golden horn on its forehead, walks past followed by her puppies who have negro's faces and horses' tails; USPUD picks up the puppies, tears them apart with his hands and waters the ground with their blood. Sword blades grow and USPUD rolls upon them. The bitch starts to howl.

Other bitches arrive with their offspring; they all throw themselves upon USPUD and tear him apart. Christ appears in the firmament; celestial music is heard; and USPUD dies devoured, crying out: "I am a martyr!"

End of the Third and Last Act.

Erik Satie ✝✝ J.P.Contamine de Latour ✝

Saints and Blessed Ones, friends of USPUD's family:

Saint Chassebaigre, the Thankless; Saint Lumore, hair's buttock; Saint Magrin, confessor; Saint Gebu, sheet's paw; Saint Glunde, three pencils; Saint Krenou, gentle rebellion; Saint Japuis, the roofer; Saint Umbeuse, green below; the Blessed Melou, the cripple; Saint Vequin, the disagreeable; Saint Purine, the shoeless.

Dedication

To the Ardent, Superhuman faith, in Jesus our divine master, of the twelve Apostles, including Judas before his deplorable treachery.

De Profundis, short form:
De Profundis clamaui ad te Domine;
Domine, exaudi uocem meam.

Prayer for the dead before Act Three
J.P. Contamine de Latour † Erik Satie ††

Dedication

To the Dissecting, Immobile and Preparatory Sainte Chapelle in Paris recently sacrileged.

Erik Satie †† J.P.Contamine de Latour †

Fidelium animae per misericordiam Dei, requiescant in pace. Amen.

J.P.Contamine de Latour † Erik Satie ††

This work was finished to our great joy the 72nd of the Works of Hermetic Contemplation, as Evening was coming on.

J.P.Contamine de Latour † Erik Satie ††

Uspud

christian ballet, in three acts, by j. p. contamine de latour.
music by erik satie.
presented at the théâtre national de l'opera, 20th. december 1892

Dedication
To the Most High, Luminous,
Permanent
Indivisibility
of the three Persons of the Holy Trinity

uspud
sole character: uspud
spirtualities: the christian church; saints, martyrs and confessors;
christ on the cross; celestial messengers of the seven orders; demonialities.

In order to understand these fragments one must take into account the conventional displacement of the keys. Here we will take that of G. I proceeded to a momentary displacement in order to dazzle the stupid.

(Hand-written note by Satie on his own copy. Private collection.)

ACT ONE

a deserted beach; in the centre, a statue; in the distance, the sea

uspud in persian dress

uspud has returned from the martyrdom of the christians and brings with him relics. he makes a pile of them at the foot of the statue and sets fire to them. the smoke that rises from them turns into seraphim, which fade into the air. there is a terrible clap of thunder; the statue falls to pieces. uspud is aghast. suddenly the sky turns white. a woman of great beauty, clad in a golden tunic with a dagger piercing her heart, appears before uspud and stretches out her arms to him. it is the christian church.

uspud, in surprise, picks up some sand and rubs his eyes with it.

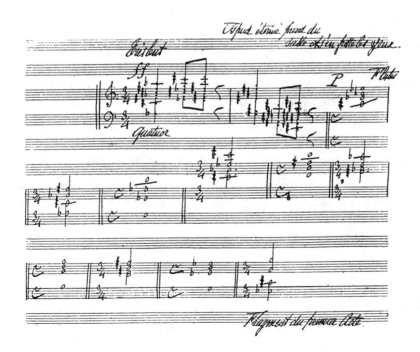

a fanfare of trumpets. an aerial parade of martyrs cursing uspud. uspud picks up stones and throws them at the christian church. the stones become balls of fire. uspud's fury. he takes up a bigger stone, which bursts with a great crash; flames rush forth and from their midst fly stars.

a great convulsion of nature.

end of the first act

ACT TWO

uspud's house

uspud beseeches his household gods.

demons come forth and instantly disappear. they take on the shape of deformed men with animal heads such as; dog, jackal, tortoise, goat, fish, lynx, tiger-wolf, ox, snipe, narwhal, sheep, antelope, ant, spider, gnu, snake, agouti, blue goat, baboon, cuckooloo, crab, albatross, pacre, ostrich, mole, secretary, old bull, red caterpillar, bonti, pogos, wild boar, crocodile, buffalo, etc.

uspud is afraid and tries to run away, but the demons surround him and knock him down; he tries to smash his head, but the walls draw back and seep blood. in the air can be seen a vision of a pagan court of justice, before which victims are tortured. uspud in his anguish calls upon heaven.

the christian church appears once more, white as snow and transparent as crystal; lotus flowers bloom beneath her feet. she draws the dagger from her chest and plunges it into uspud's; he goes into ecstasy. at the same time a vast crucifix comes from the earth and rises to heaven, drawing after it the christian church. a choir is heard of angels and archangels,

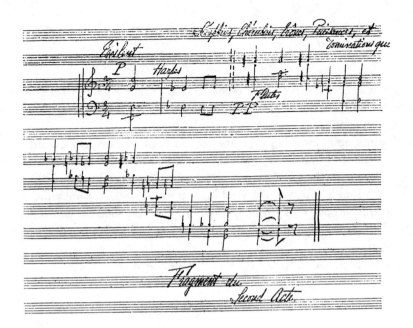

seraphim, cherubim, thrones, powers, and dominions, who sing praise to the lord on high. a great light surrounds uspud; he falls upon his knees, beating his chest. he is converted.

end of act two

ACT THREE

a mountain top; above it a crucifix

uspud, dressed in a cowl, lies prostrate before the crucifix; for a long time he prays and weeps.

when he lifts his head, the christ detaches his right arm from the cross, blesses uspud and disappears. the holy spirit is with uspud.

procession of saints; saint cleophemus spits his teeth out into his hand; saint micanar carrying her eyes on a salver; the blessed marcomir, with his legs burnt to cinders; saint induciomare with his body pierced by arrows; saint chassebaigre, confessor, in a violet robe; saint lumore with her blade; saint gebu with reddened talons; saint glunde with a wheel; saint krenou with his sheep; saint japuis with his forehead opened and doves flying forth; saint umbeuse spinning wool; the blessed melou the deformed; saint vequin the flayed; saint purine the shoeless; saint plau the fisher monk; saint benu with her axe. their voices summon uspud to martyrdom.

an unassuageable thirst for suffering comes over him. he rends his cowled cloak and is seen clothed in the white robe of the neophyte. he returns to his prayers.

62

a legion of demons rises on every side. they take on monstrous forms; black dogs with golden horns upon their brows; fishes' bodies with birds' heads and wings; giants with bulls' heads, breathing fire from their nostrils.

uspud commends his spirit to the lord, then gives himself over to the demons who tear him apart in fury.

the christian church appears, shining with clarity and escorted by two angels, bearing palms and crowns. she takes the soul of uspud in her arms and bears him towards christ who shines in the firmament.

end of act three

CURTAIN

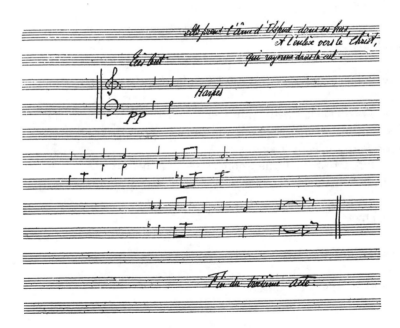

AN ACT[23]

A village square. Church. Pub. Crowd of peasants. Cheers for the elderly bridegroom.

No. 1   — Dance — the whole company.

No. 2   — Dance of the Bridegroom. Success. More cheers. Enter the young lead dancer.

No. 3   — Dance. Further cheering. Enter the Bride.

No. 4   — Dance. Cheering.

No. 5   — Dance of the bridal couple. The young lead dancer is jealous. He imparts his feelings to a young lady.

No. 6   — Dance. The crowd sets off to the Inn, leaving the Bride and the young lead. Explanations and sulking.

No. 7   — Dance. Bells ring. The crowd returns. The Bride does a crazy dance.

No. 8   — Dance. The Bride is totally indifferent.
Enter bailiffs bearing enormous warrants. A writ is served.
The Bridegroom is overwhelmed.
The bailiffs arrest the Bridegroom and lead him away.
The Bride wipes away a secret tear and lets herself be consoled by the young lead.

No. 9   — Dance. Duet.

No. 10   — Dance. Bells. Ensemble.

No. 11   — Dance. CURTAIN as they leave.

THREE LOVE POEMS[24]

1.

I'm just a grain of sand,
Still fresh, good-natured, and
A drinker, singer, laugher
for the pleasure of my lover.

Love softly, pretty girl,
your lover, for he's frail
He's but a grain of sand,
the fresh good-natured man.

2.

From birth my baldness
out of politeness
marred the trustworthiness
of my proud youthfulness.

Why such disdainfulness
from lovely Agnes?
From birth my baldness
was pure politeness.

3.

Your ornament is secret
My pretty tripping crotchet.
My lovely castanet
smokes a cigarette.

But will I win complete
devotion from my sweet?
Your ornament is secret
my pretty tripping crotchet.

erik satıe erik satıe erik satıe erik satıe erik satıe erik satıe erik satıe erik satıe erik satıe erik satıe erik satıe erik satıe erik satıe erik satıe erik satıe erik satıe erik satıe erik satıe erik satıe

Symphonic Drama in 3 Parts with Voices

_____

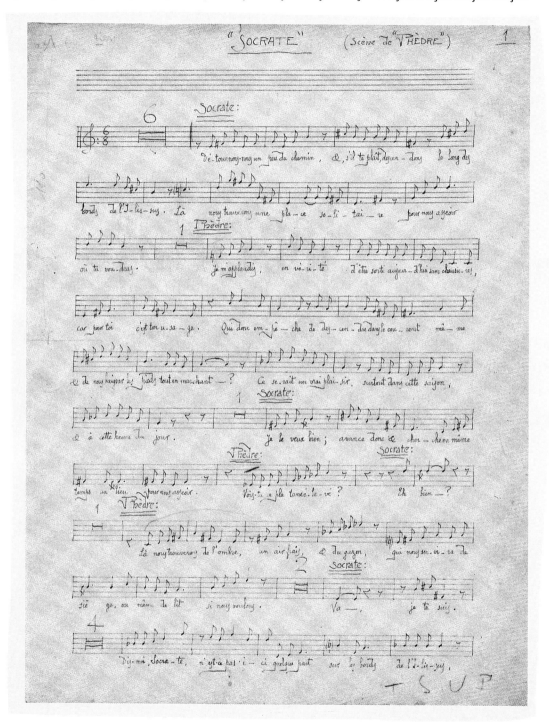

1. Portrait of Socrates[26]

ALCIBIADES: Now, my dear friends,   so as to praise Socrates,   I shall have need of comparisons: he may perhaps believe I am but joking;   but I assure you I could not be more serious.

I tell you first that he is exactly like those Silenes you see set out in sculptor's studios, and which the artists show holding a flute or pan-pipes in their hand,   but inside these small figures, when you open them, and separate the two pieces of which they are made up, you find shut up inside them statues of the lesser gods.

I will maintain also that he resembles Marsyas, the satyr...   Are you not also a player of the flute?   Yes, surely,   And greatly more surprising than Marsyas. For he charmed men with the lovely things his mouth drew from his instruments,   and nowadays indeed whoever plays his tunes can do the same;   in fact those that were played by Olympos I attribute to Marsyas, his master.

The only difference, Socrates, there is here between you and Marsyas,   is that with no instrument,   but only by speaking, you do the same thing...

For me, my friends,   did I not fear to seem to you completely tipsy,   I would swear to you under oath the extraordinary effect his speeches had on me and still do now. Listening to him, I feel my heart beating more powerfully than if I was shaken by the manic dancing of a group of corybantes.   His words bring tears to my eyes, and I see that a good number of others feel the same emotions.   So great is the influence the flute of this satyr holds over me and many others...

SOCRATES: You have just sung my praises: and now it is my turn to speak in praise of my neighbour to my right.

2. The Banks of the Ilissus

SOCRATES: Let us turn a little from the path, and if you will, walk down   along the bank of the Ilissus. There we shall find a solitary spot to sit down where you wish.

PHAEDRUS: I am very pleased, truly, to have come out today without shoes, for that is what you do usually. Who then will stop us going down right into the water and bathing our feet as we walk along. It would be really pleasant, especially at this time of year, and at this time of day.

SOCRATES: I'm happy to do that; go ahead and find at the same time a place for us to sit down.

PHAEDRUS: Do you see that tall plane tree?

SOCRATES: I do.

69

PHAEDRUS: We shall find some shade there, cool air, and some short grass, where we can sit down comfortably, or even lie if we prefer.

SOCRATES: Go on. I am coming.

PHAEDRUS: Tell me, Socrates, was it not somewhere round here, on the banks of the Ilissus, that it is said Orithyia was carried off by Boreas?

SOCRATES: So they say.

PHAEDRUS: But don't you think it was this very place? The water is so lovely, so limpid and clear, that pretty young girls could hardly find a better place to play in.

SOCRATES: And yet it was not here, but two or three stadia downstream, where one can cross the river near the temple of Artemis the Huntress. There is even an altar dedicated to Boreas.

PHAEDRUS: I will take your word for it. But tell me, honestly,   do you believe, then, this legendary adventure?

SOCRATES: Well, if I doubted it,   as many wise men do,   I would not be much embarrassed; I could be clever and just say that the North wind made her fall down from one of the rocks nearby, when she was playing with Pharmacaea, and that this death gave rise to the belief she had been carried off by Boreas;   or maybe I could say that she fell from the rock of Areopagus, since many people say it happened there....
      But tell me now   is not that the tree to which you are leading us?

PHAEDRUS: Indeed it is.

SOCRATES: By Hera, what a charming place to rest!   How broadly the mighty plane tree spreads its branches!   And this chaste-tree with its arms shooting up   and the fine shade it gives,   could one not think it is in flower, just to scent the air?
      I ask you, what could be more gracious   than this brook which runs beneath the plane tree, whose water our feet have proved is cool and fresh? This place could easily be dedicated to some nymph, and to the river Achelous, to judge by these figures and these statues.
      Just taste the air we breathe here   could anything be more delightful?   The singing of the cicadas is rather lively and feels like summer.   Above all I love this swathe of grass which gives us room to stretch out   and softly rest our heads upon this gently sloping piece of ground.
      My dear Phaedrus, you could not be a better guide.

70

3. The Death of Socrates

PHAEDO: Since Socrates had been condemned,   we had visited him without fail every day. As the public square, in which the verdict had been given,   was close beside the prison, we took to gathering there in the morning,   and there we waited,   conversing with one another, for the prison to be opened,   which was never at an early hour...

...The jailer who was usually the one to let us in   came out to us,   and told us to wait, and not come in until he called for us himself.   A few moments later he came and opened up for us. When we came in, we found Socrates, who had just been set free from his chains, and Xanthippe, whom you know, beside him holding one of her children in her arms...   Then Socrates sat up on his couch, drew up the leg which had just been released, and rubbed it with his hand   and said to us...

"How strange a thing, my friends,   is what men will call pleasure,   and what a remarkable relation it has with pain which is claimed to be its opposite!...   Is it not by enjoyment and by suffering that the body subjugates and imprisons the soul?...   I would have great difficulty persuading other men that I do not consider my present state a misfortune, since I could never convince you of it yourselves...

...You think me then, it would appear, inferior to the swan with regard to presentiment and divination.   For swans, when they feel they are about to die   sing even better on that day than they have ever sung,   from joy that they will go to meet the god they serve..."

Though many times I had admired Socrates,   I never did so as much as at this moment... I was sitting on his right hand beside the bed upon a little seat,   and he was sitting a little higher than me.   He passed his hand over my head, and lifted up my hair which hung down on my shoulders:...

"Tomorrow, Phaedo," he said,   "you will cut this fine hair, will you not?..."

...He got up and walked into the adjoining room to bathe himself;   Crito followed him and Socrates asked us to wait for him.

When he returned, he sat down on his bed and had not time to say very much to us: For the servant of the Eleven came at almost the same time,   and going up to him,   "Socrates,"   he said, "I hope I will not have to reproach you as I have to reproach the others: when I come to tell them that   by order of the magistrates   they are to drink the poison,   they fly in rage against me, and call me foul names;   but for you,   I have always found you the most brave,   the gentlest and the best of those that have ever come into this house, and at this moment I know well that I can be sure you are not angry with me   but against those who are the cause of your misfortune, whom you know well.   Now, you know what I have come to say to you.   Farewell,   try to bear with resignation what cannot be avoided."

And at the same time bursting into tears he turned away, and he withdrew.

Socrates looked at him and said:

"You too, please receive my farewell;   I will do what you say." And turning towards us: "You see," he said, "the honesty shown by this man;   all the time I have been here, he has often come to see me,   and has talked with me;   he has been the best of men   and now   look how he weeps from his heart!   Now then, Crito;   let us obey him   with good will,   and let them bring in the poison,   if it is ground;   if not, then let him grind it himself..."

Crito signed to the slave who was standing nearby. The slave went out, and after we had waited a little time, he came back with the one who was to give the poison, which he carried already ground in a cup.   As soon as Socrates saw it: "Good, my friend," he said, "But what is it I have to do? For it is you that must show me."

"Nothing more,"   the man said,   "than just walk around when you have drunk it   until you start to feel your legs getting heavy, and then you should lie down on your bed, the poison will work all by itself."

And at the same time he held out the cup...

Socrates brought the cup to his lips,   and drank with extraordinary calm and gentleness.

Till then we had almost all of us had strength enough   to hold back our tears;   but watching him drink, and after he had drunk, we could no longer restrain ourselves.   In spite of all my efforts my own tears began to flow so copiously   that I covered myself with my cloak so as to weep privately;   for it was not Socrates' misfortune I wept for, but mine, to think how great a friend I was to lose...

...Meanwhile Socrates, who was walking about   said he could feel his legs getting heavy, and he lay down on his back as the man had recommended.   At the same time the same man who had given him the poison, came close and examined for a little time his feet and legs,   and pinched his foot quite hard and asked him if he could feel it;   he said no.   Then he pinched him on his legs; and bringing his hands up higher,   he showed us that the body was growing cold and getting stiff; and touching it himself,   he said to us, that once the cold reached as far as the heart   then Socrates would leave us...

...Uncovering his face,   Socrates said: "Crito, we owe a cock to Aesculapius; do not forget to pay off this debt..."

...A short while later,   he moved convulsively;   so the man uncovered his face completely: his eyes were fixed.

Crito, as soon as he saw this, closed his mouth and his eyes...

...Such, then,   Echecrates, were the last moments of our friend...   ...the wisest and the most just of all men.

Medusa's Snare[27]

A Lyrical Comedy in one Act

by

Monsieur ERIK SATIE

with music for dancing by the same gentleman

_____

Cast, in order of appearance:

BARON MEDUSA, a very rich landowner

POLYCARPE, manservant to the Baron

ASTOLFO, Frisette's fiancé

FRISETTE, Medusa's daughter

The scene is contemporary Paris, in BARON MEDUSA's *study*

Jonah the monkey, by Erté, 1974.
Fondation Erik Satie

Scene 1

MEDUSA, *then* POLYCARPE.

MEDUSA's *study. Appropriate furniture. Upstage, a lovely big monkey stuffed by a master. Three doors: to the rear, to the courtyard, and to the garden. The monkey is a magnificent mechanical toy which the Baron had made for his personal distraction.*

MEDUSA: Am I alone?... Am I really alone?... *(He looks under all the furniture, then goes to sit down at his desk).* I like being alone, in peace and quiet. The slightest thing upsets me. Pins and needles in my shins make me vehemently ill at ease; hiccups I find most bothersome; if my slippers are too tight it readily obstructs my brain and leaves me speechless — I mean morally, of course.

Now what is this on my nose?... Oh silly me; it's my spectacles!... My golden spectacles.

> *He turns the pages of an enormous book.*

Where was I now?... Let me see... Five plus three makes eleven... take four leaves six... two plus seven makes eighteen.

That's right... *(Thinks)* God dammit... I am sixty thousand francs down!

I cannot understand it. *(He counts under his breath)*

Phew!... I am up!... I've made two billion!... *(Thumps the desk)* There must be a mistake,... a teeny little mistake...

I'll start again... *(He counts again under his breath)* For two months now I have been trying to sort out this business... I'm not getting anywhere. Why?... I ask myself fairly and squarely... *(Changing his mind)*

My agent can finish this job, my eyes are giving me trouble... my sight is getting low.

> *Enter* POLYCARPE, *wearing magnificent livery.*

POLYCARPE: Sir rang?

MEDUSA: No, I am sorry... I don't think so; ...I don't remember. My eyes are getting low.

> *He looks vacant.*

POLYCARPE: *(Going up to the Baron mysteriously)* Do you know?... I have to go out this evening... I HAVE TO. *(Imperiously)* DO YOU HEAR?

MEDUSA: *(Timidly)* This evening?

POLYCARPE: Yes... this evening... *(Cavernously)* IT IS IMPERATIVE.

MEDUSA: *(Annoyed)* This evening? It's impossible; the General is coming for dinner... Where are you going?

POLYCARPE: I am going to a billiards match. What a great match! Napoleon will be there. The billiards

Napoleon, I mean of course! ... THE REAL ONE.

MEDUSA: *(Thinking he has hit on a solution)* You could put your match off till tomorrow, couldn't you?

POLYCARPE: *(Disdainfully)* Are you mad?... Put off a billiards match!... Have you ever heard of such a thing? *(He walks out waving his arms in the air)* If Napoleon could hear you...

Exit.

MEDUSA: *(Collects himself)* I am going to warn the General, with a little telephone call bang in his ear. *(On the telephone)* Hallo!... hallo!.. Hallolololo!... Is that you, General?...

No, my dear girl, do not cut us off; do not cut off the General...

Ah! Yes!... That's right: the number?... Ninety first division.

General!... General!... I don't recognise your voice!... Have you changed your voice then?... *(Tersely)* Madam this is not the tobacconists.

What is this horse butcher's you want?... A horse has squeezed under your bed?... Give it a kick on the backside.... It's quite simple.

Come on now! What?...

Cut off again?... You've cut off the horse! I don't recognise the horse's voice! *(In a fury)* No!...

Becoming resigned

I give up!...

Enter POLYCARPE *bearing a card on an enormous tray.*

POLYCARPE: Don't see him; he will make me late... They start on time down there.

What a great match!... You ought to come... But you are too proud to go out with me, a mere worker,... a union member!

MEDUSA: *(Inspects the card from every angle)* I shall have to see him... Show him in; but tell him to walk on tiptoe for fear of waking me.

76

The Monkey's Dance (no. 1) *

*Instructions in Roman text are for the choreographer, in italic for the pianist.

Scene 2

MEDUSA; ASTOLFO.

Enter ASTOLFO. *They bow to one another ceremoniously. The Baron shows his visitor to a seat and sits down at his desk.* ASTOLFO *is very intimidated, and scarcely looks at the monkey, as if he feared being indiscreet. There is a long silence between them. They scrutinise each other.* MEDUSA *studies* ASTOLFO *carefully with a large magnifying glass.*

The monkey is suddenly still.

MEDUSA: Well, well, well... I have a feeling I have seen you somewhere before; somewhere I know... That's it.

ASTOLFO: Where would that be, sir?

MEDUSA: In my coffee grounds... I often consult them,... for fun. I am very fond of coffee, especially if it's good.

He smacks his lips.

Who recommended you to me?

ASTOLFO: General Posthumous, Sir.

MEDUSA: I have just been on the phone to him. What a fine man! He is the soul of kindness and gives away everything he has to hand.
At a parade once, a colonel presented to him a man who had not yet been punished.
The general questioned the soldier most congenially:
"So, my friend, you have never had a punishment?"
"That is correct, Sir."
"Then I shall give you one; you can have thirty days in prison."
Now that is what I call a real soldier!... What were you saying?

ASTOLFO: ?...

MEDUSA: So, you wish to marry my little Frisette?... I love Frisette very much;... which proves I have a kind heart.

ASTOLFO: Is she not your daughter?

MEDUSA: Frisette is my little foster-daughter. Oh! It's a long story. I will not tell it to you, you would not understand a thing.
Nor would I, to be honest.
Doesn't it make your spine shiver?

ASTOLFO *looks surprised.*

Don't stand there. *(*MEDUSA *gets up and moves towards* ASTOLFO*)* Go away!
If you stand there a moment longer I'll get angry.

ASTOLFO *makes to leave.*

Did I give you my photograph?

The Baron goes to his desk and comes back.

Here is one.

ASTOLFO: *(Looks at the object)* But it's an armchair!

MEDUSA: And a very good likeness... Get out now!... Off like a gun!... Come back in ten minutes... I shan't be here.

Exit ASTOLFO *joylessly.*

The Monkey's Dance (no. 2)

Scene 3

MEDUSA; FRISETTE.

MEDUSA: This little lad is quite entertaining. *(Enter* FRISETTE*)* I am being asked for your little hand,
   your wee little hand-ee.

FRISETTE: Yes, Daddy.

MEDUSA: Your fiancé is a young man who takes after General Posthumous.
   Sorry, I mean, he is recommended by General Posthumous.
   Do you know General Posthumous?

FRISETTE: Yes, Daddy.
   General Posthumous is a fine man.
   He is the soul of kindness, and gives away everything he has to hand.
   At a parade once, a colonel presented to him...

MEDUSA: I know that story.

FRISETTE: So do I. *(She laughs)*

MEDUSA: *(Severely)* A well-behaved little girl never laughs in front of her father. Now, do you want to
   get married? Don't you want to stay unmarried?
   Doesn't it bother you to leave your nice Daddy?

FRISETTE: On the contrary.

MEDUSA: Do you love your Daddy?

FRISETTE: Yes, Daddy.

MEDUSA: You are so good, you are a lovely little girl-ee.

FRISETTE: And what about my trousseau, Daddy?

MEDUSA: I shall buy you a suitcase... or a travelling bag;... you cannot go to Italy with a trousseau... A
   suitcase is, well, handier.

   Off with you now! My little she-sheep, my little harlequinny-quin-quin.

   Exit FRISETTE, *crestfallen.*

Scene 4

MEDUSA, ASTOLFO.

MEDUSA: *(Looking dreamy, as if thinking of nothing. Goes over to his desk)* Shall I get on with some work now?...

Enter ASTOLFO, MEDUSA *walks towards him.*

Am I right in thinking it's you? You have my agreement with regard to the little matter in question... Do you know?

ASTOLFO: What joy!

MEDUSA: Don't jump: you could come down on my feet... I have corns... nasty great corns.... Have you a prescription for getting rid of them?... Or to make them move somewhere else?
They wouldn't bother me if they were on my back.
Go away!... Do you know Napoleon?... The billiards one, I mean, of course...
You don't?...
Go away!
You can come back in ten minutes... I shall be a long way away.

Exit ASTOLFO, *stupefied.*

The Monkey's Dance (no. 3)

Scene 5

MEDUSA, POLYCARPE.

The Baron goes back to his desk. He writes, and lets his thoughts wander.

MEDUSA: ...I ask myself, personally... Does he love me?... I have to know. Otherwise, I shall be unable to sleep peacefully, and I shall go thirsty... I shall be a shadow of myself.

I shall ensnare him... in a clumsy snare. Those are the best ones... clumsy snares. I want a son-in-law who will really be mine; who will see only through my mouth; who will enjoy drinking in my every word; who will blend with me.

I would not like to have an egotist as a son-in-law... It would be just too ugly.

He rings, with a big bell. Enter POLYCARPE.

MEDUSA: This is a very urgent letter, take it immediately.

POLYCARPE: *(Surly)* Can't you post it?...

I am never going to be in time for my thing...

I'll be lucky if I get a seat underneath the table... You do have some strange ideas!...

It won't bring you luck!...

Exit, furious, but with dignity.

Scene 6

MEDUSA, ASTOLFO.

MEDUSA: *(Suddenly stands up; goes to the upstage door, opens it and shouts)* POLYCARPE!... POLYCARPE!...
He's gone... *(He tears out his hair and tramples on it)* Why did he go so quickly?...
He has left me!...

ASTOLFO *appears, timidly.*

MEDUSA: *(Crazily, with eyes like fireworks,* MEDUSA *addresses* ASTOLFO*)* I am a coward!...
I have just sent an anonymous letter to General Posthumous.

ASTOLFO: What do you mean?

MEDUSA: I have; I forgot to sign the letter!... He will be very upset... and will want a duel... I don't know
how to fight.
Go away!
Get out! *(Calls him back, with a change of tone)* Now tell me, my child, what do you do in life?

ASTOLFO: I work in the Department of Divorce and Accidents at Work, Sir.

MEDUSA: And you have not made any mistakes in your work? I mean, errors?

ASTOLFO: Several times, Sir: divorcees have received large disability pensions, while poor accident
victims had their marriages annulled. I am very sorry about it.

MEDUSA: It doesn't matter;... I forgive you.
Go away now!... you should take a very long trip... very long... round the neighbourhood.
It'll do you good, a world of good...
And if you meet Polycarpe, send him to me.

Exit ASTOLFO, *disillusioned. He finds his future father-in-law most surprising. He does not share his
feelings.*

The Monkey's Dance (no. 4)

Scene 7

MEDUSA, POLYCARPE, *then* ASTOLFO.

MEDUSA: I shall get back to my accounts.

> *He goes towards his desk. Enter* POLYCARPE, *looking wild.*

POLYCARPE: What a life!... It takes the patience of a cart-horse to live with you!

(*Sarcastically*) Will Sir let me go out to my match?... You have a nerve!

(*Disdainfully*) You're just a barbarian, you have no ideals... Take you away from your figures and you're good for nothing.

I thought I could make something of you, but I am abdicating, I shall leave you in your murky, musty corner. Anyway, I am getting married.

> *Enter* ASTOLFO. *He seems confused at* POLYCARPE'*s flood of rhetoric.*

You will be left all alone.

If I were you, I would be ashamed and would kill myself by shoving a stick between my ankles.

> POLYCARPE'*s indignation is at its height.*

MEDUSA: (*Notices* ASTOLFO.) Oh my God! (*To* POLYCARPE) You may leave, my friend... Thank you for what you have just revealed... confided to me.

> *Exit* POLYCARPE, *bursting with pride.*

(*The Baron addresses* ASTOLFO) He is a most good-natured creature... he's very devoted to me;... one cannot find servants like that these days.

I was there when he was born... at the age of twenty five.

ASTOLFO: So why does he answer you back like that?

MEDUSA: It's just a tic... Don't mention it to anyone... Polycarpe founded an important trades union fourteen years ago... One day when I was cross-eyed — my eyes were so bad I did not know where to put myself — Polycarpe offered to make me a member of his union, which he assured me would do me a world of good... A month later I was cured... and bald.

Out of gratitude I was obliged, under the statutes of the secret union, to grant my brother Polycarpe a degree of freedom, a degree of latitude, in performing his duties. Polycarpe had become my brother. It's rather curious, don't you think? Without my thinking, my squint had made me a socialist, via Polycarpe.

Like all weak characters, he takes advantage of it.

Shh... Shh. ..! If you so much as mention this to my daughter, she will have a headache... a terrible headache.

The doctor does not want her to have headaches. HE DOESN'T WANT HER TO! Dr. Cringe is a terrible man... quite terrible!

> MEDUSA *stretches his arms wide and puts on a deep voice.*

His belly comes out to here... It is horrible!...
Do you understand?

> ASTOLFO *is quite stupefied.*

As I was saying, my child...
Which service were you in?

ASTOLFO: Navy, Sir; I've finished, almost.

MEDUSA: Oh, so you were dressed up like my little nephew who is four years old, were you?
A sailor's suit at your age!
Get out!

> *He pushes* ASTOLFO *in front of him.*

I think there has just been a call for you... It may be about your taxes...
Out with you!

> *Exit* ASTOLFO. MEDUSA *follows him with his eye diabolically.*

The Monkey's Dance (no. 5)

Scene 8

MEDUSA, POLYCARPE.

MEDUSA: I am mortified... What can the boy think?
And the other one still keeps talking back at me!
He will snap at me in front of General Posthumous!
I have had enough. *(He calls)* Polycarpe!... Polycarpe.

> POLYCARPE *makes a monumental entrance.*

POLYCARPE: Did you ring again?

MEDUSA: Of course!... I rang with my voice... *(Pause)* I am resigning as a member of the union.

POLYCARPE: *(With authority)* You have no right to.

MEDUSA: I shall quite simply claim the right.
Our pact has been broken; and I have to tell you that if you do not behave properly towards me, I will throw you out... I will have you shot.

POLYCARPE: *(Brimming with hypocrisy)* At your service, my Lord...
His Lordship will forget about this detail will he not?
His Lordship will take pity on a father-to-be who wishes to get married?

MEDUSA: Brrr ...! Go and hide in the cellar!... At the back of the cellar!
For a man that wants to get married you are going about things very badly, Mister Polycarpe.
Married men won't be in the least flattered to have you join them. Remove yourself from my sight... for a little while.

> *Exit* POLYCARPE. *He is not the same man.*

The Monkey's Dance (no. 6)

Scene 9

MEDUSA, ASTOLFO, FRISETTE, POLYCARPE.

MEDUSA: I have subjugated him.

The Baron checks the thermometer..

My sight is getting so low! It has gone down six degrees since this morning!...

ASTOLFO appears.

Careful! Now's the time to test him with my snare.

MEDUSA mesmerises ASTOLFO.

(Out of the blue) Can you dance on one eye?... your left eye?

ASTOLFO: *(Choking with surprise)* ?

MEDUSA: *(Behaving as if he was a hypnotist. Brusquely)* I asked you if you can dance on one eye?... on your left eye?

He pokes his finger in his right eye.

That one?

ASTOLFO: *(In a voice strangled with mental confusion)* No.

MEDUSA: *(As if to himself)* All right, he is a good, simple fellow... *(His face glows with pleasure)* I am very pleased with your answer, you are a loyal man, and neither devious nor tortuous.

ASTOLFO: Just because I cannot dance on one eye?

MEDUSA: No, no! *(Sententiously)* From now on, I shall trust you, you would undoubtedly go to your death for me, without telling a soul about it. Embrace me now, my boy ... harder.

He looks at him with idiotic sweetness.

Right now, you look like Voltaire. My Goodness... You have the same crooked legs as him!... If I should die, what would you do?

ASTOLFO: *(Without much conviction)* I should dress in black and go to your funeral, Sir.

MEDUSA: Then you love me! *(He hugs him paternally)* Hug me... tighter... again! It would be hard for you to live without me, wouldn't it? You want to make me happy, don't you? Only to make me happy.

Enter FRISETTE very modestly.

(Introducing her) My daughter.

(Introducing ASTOLFO*)* My son-in-law. *(He goes on)* You must realise that you are entering an illustrious house. My family is an old family which has lent its name to an invertebrate animal of the acephalous class — an excellent class!

This animal lives in the sea.

I will introduce you to it... You will like it, won't you?

ASTOLFO: *(Deeply moved)* Yes, Sir.

MEDUSA: *(Taking* ASTOLFO*'s hand in his)* You are so good... so very good... too good.

I used to have a portrait of it, painted by Bonnat; but I took it away, my daughter was afraid of it. She treats it with deference, don't you Frisette?

FRISETTE: Yes, Papa.

MEDUSA: My dear little children!... The General will be so happy to see you together!...

He goes over to the monkey.

Jonah will be happy too. He is still the best man among us.

He bursts into tears like a fool.

FRISETTE: Oh papa!

ASTOLFO: Oh Sir!

They hug the monkey. MEDUSA *puffs out his chest outrageously. He pulls himself together.*

FRISETTE: *(Stroking the monkey)* Good old Jonah.

ASTOLFO: *(Who does not understand a thing)* Good old Mister Jonah.

MEDUSA: *(To* ASTOLFO, *indicating* FRISETTE*)* Love her as you love me.

Do not forget that she is my daughter, and that you owe her to me.

(Very serious) Lie down on the floor, my children; I shall bless you myself with my own hands... That will warm me up; my hands are frozen. *(The betrothed pair hesitate; they do not know what to do. They are disgusted by the idea of lying on the floor)*

POLYCARPE: *(Announcing in a magnificent voice)* General Posthumous of Knockabout;... Colonel Polecat;... and Mr Knee... military administrator!

MEDUSA: *(Suddenly scared stiff)* We must run! ... *(He heads for a side door)* Let's get out of here!... THEY WANT TO FIGHT!

The Baron runs away, followed by FRISETTE *and* ASTOLFO. POLYCARPE *stands aside to make way for the General, the Colonel, and the plain Mister.*

The Monkey's Dance (no. 7)

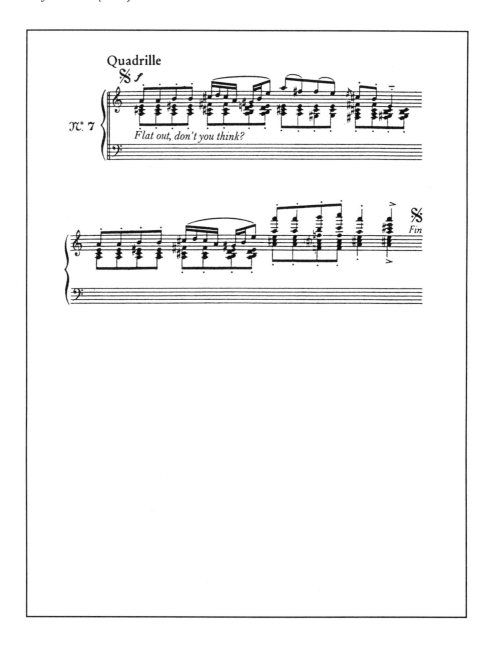

CURTAIN

EPISTLE THE FIRST OF ERIK SATIE TO CATHOLIC ARTISTS AND TO ALL CHRISTIANS[28]

My brothers;

We live in a troubled time when Western society, daughter of the Apostolic Roman Catholic Church, is invaded by the shades of ungodliness, a thousand times more barbarous than in the days of Paganism, and seems near to perishing. Only with regret can we watch men offending God each day, through their disregard for the divine precepts of the Gospel, and distancing themselves from the fervour, the continence, of Holy observance and pious customs; We are saddened to see them listening to those who openly display their diabolical works and their lies.

We rebuke them that they commit pride, impenitence and malice to the highest degree, instead of mortifying, by the offer of their sufferings, all that remains earthly in them; and We are unhappy no longer to find them battling for the glory of God, the honour of the church, and the edification of the public. Our Christian heart, which dares to attribute to these causes the evils which afflict Us, was moved to see the unhappiness of so many souls on the path to eternal damnation; and it has drawn from the infinite grace of O.L.J.C. the ardent desire to work for their sanctification, by the means most appropriate to restore Holy Religion which the wicked trample underfoot, and the Arts, which are its most sublime expression.

We have therefore resolved, in accordance with our conscience, and trusting in the mercy of God, to raise in the metropolis of this Frankish nation, which through so many centuries bore the glorious title of Elder daughter of the Church, a Temple worthy of the Saviour, LEADER and redeemer of peoples; We shall make of it a refuge where Catholicism, and the Arts which are indissolubly linked to it, shall grow and prosper, sheltered from all profanation, and at the full expansion of their purity, which the efforts of the Evil One cannot sully.

After mature reflection we have given to this asylum of enlivened Faith the name of Metropolitan Church of Art, and placed it under the divine invocation of Jesus Leader. The first inestimable expressions of affectionate gratitude and Christian approval, which a large number of Our brothers has chosen to offer Us, have filled Our heart at once with ineffable joy, and with the fortifying seed of courage to resist the traps which Hell may place in our path.

We plead with you therefore, My Brothers, in the name of Humanity's Salvation, as likewise of Our own Salvation, to join with Us for the triumph of Our-Holy-Mother-the-Church, in the purification of the Faith and of the Arts, which is one of the ways in which Providence calls us to her; and we kiss You in the Peace and Brotherhood of J.C.O.L.

Given in Paris in October 1893, the 15th.

TO M. CAMILLE SAINT-SAËNS[29]

Erik Satie
Chapel Master
of the Metropolitan Church of Art
of Jesus the Guide
to M. Camille Saint-Saëns
For my indignation and for his improvement
Paris, the 17th of the month of May of '94

Sir,
I presented myself for your approbation
to be chosen in succession
to M. Charles Gounod
within your Company.
I was not yielding to a mad presumption,
but to conscience of my duty.
The sentiment of justice,
or failing that, simple urbanity,
led Me to believe My candidacy,
allowed by God, would be accepted by you.
I was greatly afflicted
to see you forget
for the sake of vulgar preferences
solidarity in Art.
May those of my competitors
to whom you dealt the same outrage humiliate themselves;
I remain strong in My right
to be recognised, be it merely as existing.
You can reproach Me only for one thing:
That you do not know Me
as I know you.
If I am far from you,
You should not be without knowledge of Me.
Judging Me from a distance and so deciding,
you have committed the act of a reprobate
and incurred hell fire.
Your aberration can only derive
from your weakness before Secular ideas
and your ignorance of God,
the direct cause of your Aesthetic abasement.
I forgive you in the name of Jesus Christ
and embrace you in the grace of God.

Erik Satie
6, Rue Cortot

FROM THE *CARTULAIRE*[30]

My lordly soul is brimming with noble resentment. One does not savour sufficiently the state of poverty, and this is a sign of the gravest disorder. Poverty comes from God and cannot rightly be renounced without disobedience to him. As for those that dare to complain of misfortune and fear not to find relief, they are the ferment of corruption; they would destroy the inequalities that ensure the equilibrium of the world, and prepare dire cataclysms.

There is no more charity; giving is for pride, to satisfy the most despicable vanity and ambition. Titled ladies offer the most detestable example. I should fail altogether if I did not reprimand them severely. Under the banner of charity, they organise unhealthy pleasures; their feasts and gatherings are veritable courts of prostitution. They accept among them harlots; they welcome them, give them consideration, adopt their manner, their bearing, and their morals. Their indignity deserves an ignominious death.

There are others who taint the harmony of human conditions for the sake of a misleading reputation. For example, there is a certain dame Gebbart or Ghebard, better known under the name of Séverine,[31] who trawls through the public broadsheets infirmities worthy of respect and discretion. I am astonished that she should be allowed to raise her voice; woman has no business in public affairs, her place is in the home. What is dame Gebbart or Ghebard doing, far from her spouse and children? She garbs herself in the glow of sham love for the poor, though for long she roused them to rebellion and hatred, to the most deadly passions. Christians must keep far from such intermediaries, to accomplish their pious works; or they will not count in their favour. God cherishes for such ministry his servants who wear monastic robes.

I have also to remonstrate against the poor. They allow themselves indecent aspirations and it is blameworthy. Their state is their path to salvation, and from it they shall not turn away. Jesus was born poor to teach them resignation and silence, and not to inspire them to incredible recriminations. Their misfortune is a vast and honourable blessing, it brings them, sinners though they be, close to the Son of God. What more, then, do they want? What are the grotesque rumours and mad claims that rise from every side, but the echoes of bitterness, and of senseless hatred? And yet, let them not hope to realise their reckless views. If they should try, am I not there to prevent them, and can any resist him who is accompanied by the Destinies?

François de Paule,[32] *Lord of the Marches of Savoy*

Monsieur Sadi dans sa maison
Il songe

WHAT I AM[33]

Anyone will tell you that I am not a musician. They are right.

From the beginning of my career I immediately classified myself as a phonometrographer. My work is pure phonometrics. If you look at *The Son of the Stars*, or *Pieces in the Form of a Pear, In Horse Dress* or the *Sarabands*, you can see that no musical idea presided over the creation of these works. Scientific thought is predominant.

In fact it gives me more pleasure to measure a sound than to hear one. With my phonometer in hand, I work with joy and with assurance.

What is there that I have not weighed or measured? The whole of Beethoven, the whole of Verdi, etc. It is most curious.

The first time I used a phonoscope, I examined a middling-sized B flat. I can assure you, I have never seen anything more revolting. I called my servant to have him look.

On the phono-scales a common or garden F sharp gave a reading of 93 kilogrammes. It issued from a decidedly large tenor whose weight I took.

Do you know about cleaning sounds? It is a rather dirty business. Spinning them out is cleaner; learning to classify them is very finicky and requires good eyesight. But this brings us into the field of phonotechnics.

In the case of sonorous explosions which are often so unpleasant, a piece of cotton placed in the ears softens them most conveniently, for itself. This brings us into the field of pyrophony.

I used a kaleidophone-recorder to write my *Cold Pieces*. It took seven minutes. I called my servant to have him hear them.

I think I can say that phonology is superior to music. It is more varied. It gives a better return on investment. My fortune is based on it.

In any case, with a motodynamophone, a phonometrist of quite mediocre capacities can take down more sounds than the most expert musician, given the same amount of time and effort. It is thanks to this that I have written so much.

The future therefore lies with philophony.

PERFECT ENTOURAGE[34]

To live surrounded by glorious works of Art is one of the greatest joys that one can feel. Among the precious monuments of human thought with which the modesty of my fortune has led me to choose to share my life, I would like to mention a magnificent fake Rembrandt, generously and profoundly executed, which is so good to finger with the tips of one's eyes, like a fat fruit that is too green.

I could also show you in my study, a canvas of unquestioned beauty, the object of universal admiration: the delightful "Portrait attributed to an unknown artist."

Have I told you about my copy of Teniers?[35] It is an adorable, sweet creation, as rare as you will find.

Are these not divine gemstones, set in hardwood? Yes?

But then, what surpasses these masterly works? What crushes them with the formidable weight of inspired majesty? What makes them pale before its blinding light? A fake Beethoven manuscript, a sublime apocryphal symphony by the master — bought by me, religiously, ten years ago, I think.

This still unknown 10th symphony is one of the most sumptuous works of the grandiose composer. Its proportions are as vast as a palace; its ideas are cool and shady; its developments precise, and right.

This symphony had to exist: the number 9 is not properly Beethovian. He liked the decimal system: "I have ten fingers" he explained.

Some of those who have come humbly to imbibe this masterpiece with meditative, dedicated ears, thought without good reason that the conception was inferior for Beethoven, and said so. They even went further than that.

Beethoven cannot, in any circumstances, be inferior to himself. Even in the smallest detail, his technique and form are oracular. The word rudimentary cannot be applied to him. He is not intimidated by the forgery attributed to his artistic person.

Do you think a long-famous athlete, whose strength and agility have been acknowledged in public triumphs, is demeaned if he carries with ease a simple bunch of tulips and jasmine? Or lessened, if he is also assisted by a child?

You will hardly disagree with that.

MY THREE CANDIDATURES[36]

A luckier man than me, Gustave Charpentier[37] is a member of the Institut de France. May I offer him here and now the fond applause of an old friend.

I was three times a candidate for the Delicate Gathering: for Ernest Guiraud's[38] seat, Charles Gounod's seat, and Ambroise Thomas' seat.

MM. Paladilhe, Dubois and Lenepveu[39] were preferred to me, for no very good reason. And this caused me much pain.

Though I am not very observative, I had the impression that the Precious Members of the Académie des Beaux-Arts were treating my person with a degree of pig-headedness and wilfulness that bordered on calculated obstinacy. And this caused me much pain.

At the time of M. Paladilhe's election my friends said to me: "Let it pass: later he will vote for you, Maître. His voice will carry great weight." I received neither his vote, nor his voice, nor his weight. And this caused me much pain.

At the time of M. Dubois' election, my friends said to me: "Let it pass: later there will be two of them to vote for you, Maître. Their voice will carry great weight." I received neither their vote, nor their voice, nor their weight. And this caused me much pain.

I withdrew. M. Lenepveu thought it in good taste to take a seat that was intended for me, and did not see what bad manners it was to do so. He blithely sat down in my place. And this caused me much pain.

With sadness again, I should mention my old companion in the struggle, M. Emile Pessard.[40] I noticed several times that he went about it very badly, with no subtlety, not even the simplest of tricks. *He does not know,* and one sees all too well that *he does not know.* Poor dear gentleman! How hard it will be for him to find a place, to worm his way into a bosom so unkind to him, so unwelcoming, so inhospitable to him! I have watched him heaving away for the last twenty years with this thankless, cheerless, gloomy object; while the artful cronies in the Palais Mazarin watch him in amazement, surprised by his incompetent tenacity and his pale impotence.

And this causes me much pain.

THEATRICAL THINGS[41]

I have always thought of writing an opera with the following particular subject:

At that time, I was doing a lot of alchemy. Alone in my laboratory one day, I was having a rest. Outside the sky was pale, leaden, sinister: quite horrible!

I was sad, without understanding why; almost fearful, for no apparent reason. I had the bright idea of cheering myself up by counting slowly on my fingers from one to two hundred and sixty thousand.

I did so; all that happened was that I got very bored. I got up, fetched a magic nut, and placed it gently in an alpaca-bone box adorned with seven diamonds.

Immediately a stuffed bird took flight; a monkey's skeleton ran off; a sow's skin climbed the wall. Then night came to cover the objects and destroy all shapes.

But someone knocked at the back door, the one near the Median talismans, which were sold to me by a Polynesian maniac.

What is it? O Lord! Abandon not thy servant! He has certainly sinned but he repents. Forgive him, I implore you!

And then the door opens, opens, opens like an eye: a formless silent being comes closer and closer, and closer. Not a drop of sweat remains in my terrified body; and besides, I am very, very thirsty.

A voice comes out of the shadows:

"Sir, I think I am clairvoyant."

I do not know this voice. It says:

"Sir, it is me; it *is* me."

"Who do you mean, you?," I say anxiously.

"Me, your man-servant. I think I am clairvoyant. Did you just gently place a magic nut in an alpaca-bone box adorned with seven diamonds?"

I choked, but could only reply:

"Yes, my friend. How did you know?"

He sidles gloomily up to me, black in the darkness. I can feel him trembling. He is probably frightened I will fire a gun at him.

With a hiccup like a little child, he mumbles:

"I saw you through the keyhole."

THE MUSICIAN'S DAY[42]

An Artist must regulate his life.

This is the precise timetable of my daily acts.

I rise: at 07.18; inspired: from 10.23 to 11.47. I lunch at 12.11 and leave the table at 12.14.

Constitutional ride around my estate: from 13.19 to 14.53. Further inspiration: from 15.12 to 16.07.

Various activities (fencing, reflection, immobility, visits, contemplation, dexterity, swimming, etc.): from 16.21 to 18.47.

Dinner is served at 19.16 and ends at 19.20. Followed by symphonic readings, aloud: from 20.09 to 21.59.

I retire with regularity at 22.37. Once a week, I wake up with a start at 03.19 (on Tuesdays).

I eat only white victuals: eggs, sugar, grated bones; the fat of dead animals; veal, salt, coconuts, chicken cooked in white water; fruit mould, rice, turnips; camphorised sausage, pasta, cheese (cream), cotton salad and certain kinds of fish (without the skin).

I have my wine boiled, and drink it cold with fuschia juice. I am a hearty eater; but never speak while eating, for fear of strangling.

I breathe with care (a little at a time). I very rarely dance. When walking, I hold my sides, and stare fixedly behind me.

I look very serious, and if I laugh, it is never on purpose. I always apologise, and do so most affably.

I sleep with only one eye; I sleep very hard. My bed is round, with a hole to put my head through. Every hour a servant takes my temperature and gives me a new one.

I have subscribed for many years to a fashion magazine. I wear a white cap, white stockings, and a white waistcoat.

My doctor has always told me to smoke. He adds to his advice:

"You should smoke, my friend: for if you don't, someone else will smoke in your place."

INTELLIGENCE AND MUSICALITY AMONG ANIMALS[43]

The intelligence of animals is beyond denial. But what does man do to improve the mental state of these submissive fellow-citizens? He gives them a mediocre, interrupted, incomplete education, which a child would not choose for itself; and the dear little person would be quite right. This education consists largely of developing the atavistic instinct for cruelty and vice which persists in most individuals. There is never any mention in this teaching programme of art, or literature, or natural or social sciences, or other subjects. Carrier pigeons are not prepared for their mission at any time, by an acquaintance with geography; fish are kept from studying oceanography; cattle, sheep, calves are completely ignorant about the systematic layout of the modern slaughterhouse, and have no idea of their nutritional role in the society man has built for himself.

Few animals have the benefit of human education. Dogs, mules, horses, donkeys, parrots, blackbirds and one or two others are the only animals which receive anything resembling an education. And then it is more like simple up-bringing than anything else.

If you will compare this education for a moment to the instruction provided by our universities to a young human bachelor, you will see that it is worthless and can do nothing to enlarge or make accessible the knowledge the animal has acquired through its work, performed with such application. But musically! Horses have learnt to dance; spiders have sat under a piano the whole way through long concerts, specially organised for them by a respected master of the keyboard.

And besides that? Nothing. Here and there we are told about the musicality of starlings, or the crow's ability to remember tunes, or the owl's ingenious harmony when it accompanies itself by beating on its belly, a purely artificial means giving meagre polyphony.

As for the nightingale which is endlessly referred to, its musical knowledge is enough to make the most ignorant listener shrug his shoulders. Not only is its voice not trained, but it knows nothing about keys, or pitch, or mode, or rhythm. It may well be gifted. Quite possibly; in fact, quite certainly. But one can say firmly that its artistic development is not on a par with its natural gifts, and that the voice it is so proud of, is only a very inferior instrument which in itself is useless.

A SIMPLE QUESTION[44]

Which do you prefer:
Music or Ham?
It seems this is a question one should ask oneself when the *hors d'oeuvres* arrive.
In many places sweet and excellent silence has been replaced by bad music. It is thought smart by most people to hear falsely pretty things, and listen to silly, vaguely churchy ritornellos, while they drink a beer or try on a pair of trousers; to appear to appreciate the sonorous tribute of basses and bassoons, and other ugly-pipes, while thinking of nothing at all.

Peuh! All this is pretty painful for a man of my age; this kind of musical Dufayelisation[45] makes me choke.

The remedy? Heavy taxes; terrible vexations; severe repression. Cruel torture, even.

Should people be allowed just to go ahead and make our poor life ugly?

Look at these publishers with no human dignity, no shame; look at the grotesque arrangements in which they dress up the purest works, which have been submitted to them, confided to them, and which they deck out with their filth. Take one or two catalogues of modern works, some of the most delicate ones, and look at what these filthy creatures subject them to.

Just wait, they will be shamed yet.

"Trade!" You may say.

"Business!," you say again.

Well! It is all pretty painful for a man of my age; this kind of musical Dufayelisation and putrid money-grubbing makes me choke.

Which do you prefer:

Music or Ham?

HIDDEN CORNERS OF MY LIFE[46]

The origin of the Saties

may reach back into the mists of time. Yes... This, I may say, I cannot either prove or disprove...

However, I suppose that this family did not belong to the Nobility *(even Papal)*, that its members were good modest serfs, which in the past was an honour and a pleasure *(for the serf's good lord, I mean)*. Yes.

What the Saties did in the Hundred Years' War, I do not know; nor do I have any details of their attitude or the role they played in the Thirty Years' War *(one of our finest wars)*.

May the memory of my ancient ancestors rest in peace. Yes...

Let's move on. I will come back to that.

As far as I am concerned, I was born in Honfleur *(Calvados)*, in Pont-l'Evêque arrondissement, on 17th May 1866.... which makes me a fifty-year old, as good a title as any.

Honfleur is a little town washed together, and in connivance, by both the poetic waters of the Seine and the stormy waters of the Channel. The inhabitants *(Honfleurais)* are very polite and pleasant. Yes...

I stayed in this city up to the age of twelve (1878) and came to settle in Paris... I had a quite unremarkable childhood and adolescence, with no features worth recording in serious writings. So, I will not talk about them.

Let's move on. I will come back to that.

106

I am sizzlingly keen at this point to give you my personal details *(list of physical characteristics, those which I can properly speak about, of course)*: Hairs and eyebrows, dark chestnut coloured; eyes, grey *(probably flecked)*; forehead, frowning; nose, long; mouth, average; chin, broad; face, oval. Height: 1m. 67 cm.

This identification document dates from 1887, when I performed my voluntary service with the 33rd Infantry regiment in Arras *(Pas-de-Calais)*. It would not do for me today.

I am afraid I cannot show you my fingerprints *(very digital)*. Yes. I do not have them on me, and these curious reproductions are not pretty to behold *(they look like a combination of Vuillermoz and Laloy)*.[47]

Let's move on. I will come back to that.

After a fairly short adolescence I became an ordinarily drinkable, more or less passable young man, nothing more. It was at this point in my life that I began to think and write musically. Yes.

What a terrible idea!... a truly terrible idea!

Indeed, I rapidly developed an unpleasant habit of originality *(very original)*, which was out of context, anti-French, against nature, etc.

Life therefore became so unbearable for me that I resolved to retire to my estate and spend my days in an ivory tower — or was it some other metal? *(very metallic)*

That is how I acquired a taste for misanthropy; I cultivated hypochondria; I was the most melancholic human being *(very leaden)*. I was painful to behold — even through a guaranteed gold pince-nez. Yes.

And all this was brought about by Music. That art has done me more bad than good: it has ruined my relationship with many excellent, truly honourable, more than distinguished, "respectable" people.

Let us move on. I will come back to that.

Personally, I am neither good nor bad. I oscillate, I could say. So I have never really done harm to anyone — nor good, either.

And yet, I have many enemies, faithful enemies, of course. Why? This is largely due to the fact that they do not know me, or know me only at second-hand, by hear say *(the falsest of falsehoods)* in fact.

No man can be perfect. I bear them no grudge: they are the principal victims of their lack of awareness and perspicacity... Poor people!...

I do pity them.

Let us move on. I will come back to that.

(To be continued)

M. SADI

ON BEING DIZZY[48]

Once when I was in the country with a friend, we were talking about dizziness, and my friend had never experienced it.

I gave him several demonstrations of dizziness, without the slightest effect. My friend could not conceive of the agony one can feel at the sight of a roofer high on a roof. At every instance I put forward, my friend shrugged his shoulders, which is neither very polite nor very friendly.

Suddenly I caught sight of a blackbird which had just landed on a branch, a high branch, an old branch. The creature's position was highly perilous... the wind was swinging the aged branch that the poor thing clung to with clenched fingers.

I turned to my companion, and said: "Look up there — this blackbird makes me dizzy and gives me goose-pimples. Quickly, let us put a mattress under the tree, for if the bird loses its balance, it will surely break its back."

And do you know what my friend answered?

He merely said, quite coolly: "You are a pessimist."

It is not easy to make people change their mind.

AMBROISE THOMAS[49]

His art? I will not speak about that, if you do not mind, but restrict myself here to giving a few vague impressions.

Why should I talk about his so curious prosody? Philine sings: *I a-am the blonde Titania;* Laertes says to us: *Lovely woman, have pity o-on us.* That is quite enough.

But where have I gone and left my umbrella?[50]

His great age singled him out to represent the musical grandeur of France. He was accepted without protest, as indeed he was without joy. It was a matter of indifference.

Luckily that umbrella was not very expensive.

The place he filled in the official musical world appeared considerable, but did not enlarge his esteem in the eyes of artists: it was rather like the splendid function of a general in command of an army division, very visible and very honorary. That is pretty good, you will say; which is fine by me.

I must have left my umbrella in the lift.

Physically, he was tall, lean, surly: a sort of scarecrow. He obstinately drew attention to himself by not putting his arms, which he held against his sides, through the arms of his copious, positively vast, overcoat, which made him look as if he was eternally carrying one of his friends on his back. It was his way of having long hair.

My umbrella must be very worried to have lost me.

Maybe his arms were too big; or perhaps he could not move them, do you think? I do not think so:

erik satie erik satie erik satie erik satie erik satie erik satie erik satie erik satie erik satie erik satie erik satie erik satie erik satie erik satie erik satie erik satie

his frock-coat and waistcoat clothed him in the long-established manner, being clearly both formal and black.

He died heaped with honours.

THE MUSICIANS OF MONTMARTRE[51]

You may find this rather brief, but I do not mind.

Two or three hundred years ago, very few of the present musicians on the Butte existed, their names were unknown to the public at large, or even small. All that has changed, especially — it seems — over the last ten years.

I would have liked, by means of talismanic practices which are beyond the reach of brucolacs,[52] to accomplish at least once what has always been my greatest wish: to perform a commemorative passage which flies the flag for the most respected musicians in Montmartre.

But then, troubled by a scruple which I attribute quite simply to the exquisite shyness I have attained through the salutary practice of inwardness, I saw that I would have to withdraw — to my regret, I need hardly say — from a task which I consider succulent, for in spite of my intelligence I am quite unable to express in the tight space available to me here, the full majesty of my thinking and my subject: and I resolved to advise the passer-by in Montmartre that he can easily attend — if he pays, of course — a few evenings in some of the splendid cabarets assembled on this marvellous sort of promontory, so as to have an almost photographic idea of what I should be writing here.

There he will hear with his own ears, or others', vibrations so rich in taste that he will exclaim for himself: "The fact that music gives no pleasure to the deaf, even those who are mute, is no reason for ignoring it."

I withdraw, in all simplicity.

[ALIBI][53]

Perhaps I was rather fierce.

Too bad! When it comes down to it, I do not regret a thing.

I just hope I will not have trouble with the police. The police do not like disappearing; they don't understand about magic. I shall be put in prison; in an unhealthy, airless prison, with nothing to do, no exercise. I shall lie on my mat, & not live my life.

No one will come to see me.

I shall probably be there a long time. I shall not be able to go to cafés, or hunting, or to my lawyer, or on the bus, or fishing in Montreuil, or to the theatre, or to the races, or bathing at the seaside with

110

the family.

I shall lose all my contacts. How little luck I have!

And then, I shall have to choose a lawyer, a good lawyer who will have to be paid a lot.

This really is fun!

But... but... I have an alibi — a little tiny teetsy-weetsy alibi — I think: can I not say quite simply that I was beside myself & and a thousand miles from imagining I might be committing a crime? That is a serious alibi; & it is not at all complicated!

I am saved!

Saved from having my bones ankylosed by stupid imprisonment!

I am my own saviour and give myself a deserved vote of thanks. In fact, I am due a reward of twenty five francs.

I shall go and collect it.

Waiter! my hat, my coat & my stick!

[DISPATCH]⁵⁴

Stockholm, 12 February 1918

The news from Petrograd is not reassuring, but leads us to expect calm to return. Twenty regiments of Cossacks are without Cassocks. Rada has had her portrait painted. Since the land was redistributed, potatoes have become inedible. They refuse to pay thumb tacks and run up and down the avenues yelling. Rada's portrait exploded, on Thursday evening.

I am told the Red guards drink wine that same colour. This morning the sun got up and went straight back to bed. There is a rumour the Cossacks have found the Cossacks' cassocks. It is forbidden from now on for night watchmen to stay up at night. In the main streets, maximalists slit open the bellies of sacks of gold, or strangle them. Yesterday, the news from the South was warmer; from the North, very cold.

The Soviet of Priests is having churches razed with razors once a week. Rada will dance this evening for the white guards. As a precaution the papers have stopped firing cannon & will fire off only one copy. The fire-guards have rebelled.

The "Russian Invalid" declares that Rada is to be married. All the banks opened last Monday at midnight. Trotsky has been run down by a hansom cab. Petrograd has gone back to the way it looked before the war; & the theatres play skittles from morn till night.

The banks have just closed. Trotsky has set off for Brest-Litovsk taking Rada with him. The Soviet of Priests has issued a revision: churches must let their beards grow. Last night, watchmen stayed up all night. Today, the sun did not get up at all. The trains are packed with potatoes going back South. Ukraine refuses to divide the land into more than a thousand pieces. The government has fallen into the hands of the potatoes.

THE WIRES

THE TABLE[55]

Personally, I have always had a lively admiration, an unmitigated admiration for the Culinary Art. The *"pleasures of the table"* are far from displeasing to me — on the contrary; & for *"the table"* I have a sort of respect — or even more.

Whether round or square, I connect it with *"holy service"* & it impresses me like a grand altar (or grand hotel — even a *"Terminus"* or a *"Continental,"* I venture to say). Yes.

For me, eating is like homework — pleasant homework — holiday homework, of course; & I make a point of doing this homework with sustained exactness and attention.

I am endowed with a good appetite, and eat for myself, but without selfishness or bestiality. In other words, I *"do better with a knife and fork than on a horse"* — though I am quite a good horseman.

But that is another story, as Mr. Kipling so rightly said.

At meals, my role has a certain importance: I am a dinner-guest, as others, at the theatre, are members of the audience. Yes. A member of the audience has a well-defined role: he listens & thinks; the diner eats & drinks. It adds up to the same thing — in spite of all the differences between the two roles. Yes.

Dishes on which are lavished calculated virtuosity and studious thoroughness are not the ones which make the strongest claim on my *"gastronomic"* attention. In Art, I like simplicity; the same goes for cookery. I am more inclined to applaud a perfectly roasted leg of lamb than a subtle concoction of meat *concealed beneath the clever make-up applied by a master of sauces* — if you will permit the image.

But that is another story.

Among my memories as a DINER, I cannot forget the pleasant lunches I had over a number of years at the home of my old friend Debussy,when he was living in the Rue Cardinet. The memory of these charming meals is fresh in my mind.

Eggs and lamb chops provided the bill of fare for these friendly occasions. But what eggs & what chops they were!... I still lick my lips over them — inwardly, as you can guess.

Debussy — who cooked these eggs & chops himself — had the secret (*the most absolute secret*) of preparing them. It was all gracefully washed down with a delicious white Bordeaux which produced a touching effect that was suitably conducive to the joys of friendship and of life far from the *"Double Fogies,"* the *"Mummies"* & other *"Old Chestnuts"* — those scourges of Humanity & the *"poor world."*

But that is yet another story.

BOOK-LOVING[56]

Selling, buying books... what a treat it must be, and what pleasure I have visiting my bookseller friends Adrienne Monnier and Sylvia Beach![57]

The first of these dear friends founded her shop in the middle of the war (the Great War); the second set up two years ago under the protection of the magnificent Shakespeare. They are both, to my mind, examples of courage. I often go by for a "little five minute chat" — and stay for hours. It reminds me of my friend Bailly's charming bookshop in the Rue de la Chaussée d'Antin (La Librairie de l'Art Indépendant).[58]

A distant memory, but sweet to recall.

Yes, it was a charming bookshop, the Librairie de l'Art Indépendant.

It was a haunt of the "young writers" of the day, and one or two musicians used to meet and chat there informally: Debussy, Chausson[59] — among others. We could be sure there of the most sensitive possible reception; and I will never forget the intimate charm of the books, any more than the image will ever leave me of that fine man "dear Bailly."

So, when my friend Pierre Trémois told me he was starting a bookshop, I jumped for joy — I almost tripped. It was good news to me — very good news; I could see myself already enjoying a thousand delights in which browsing had a significant part to play.

Isn't a bookshop, to some extent, a temple to Browsing? I think an "ensemble" of books makes us disposed to reach this "section" of the Unconscious — or at least enables that part to open its petals.

What a curious seduction! Don't we often browse along the riverside bookstalls in thoroughly bad weather, on our feet with rain-soaked shoes and the wind in our faces?

No matter! in front of us are books, which invite us to relax and stroke them with our eyes — to lose ourselves in them, blissfully — and look down on the base ties which attach us to ancient human Misery.

My friend Pierre Trémois loves books; he knows their merits and appreciates particularly their personal qualities. His affection is quite impartial and extends as much to old books as to just published youngsters; and he is an accurate guide for book lovers who ask his advice.

His shop will be cool and shady, warm and intimate — depending on the time of year; it will conjure up the Past and let us glimpse the Future. I say: — "My dear Trémois, I will often be round to visit you."

ON READING[60]

There are several ways of reading…. to oneself; to others — or at least, to someone else.

Reading "to oneself" is internal — as internal as can be; while reading "to others," or to someone else, being (generally) done aloud, is external — as external as can be.

Reading to oneself is a game; art does not come into it. In contrast, reading aloud is so difficult. If you please, we shall take a look at this interesting category.

Not many people know how to read aloud: it is, in fact, an art. Actually (this is in parenthesis) I have always wondered how the "reader"[61] reads at the Comédie Française. The good man must read really well! Prestigiously of course. But... does he read aloud? That is the question.

To start with, one does well to read aloud to only a single listener — perhaps someone on the deaf side — slightly hard of hearing, shall we say. This will make one bold — a little "cheeky"; one becomes far more assured before such a "neutral," inferior listener.

In this case, a good reader aims never to intimidate his single listener. He encourages him: speaks to him politely, without bitterness — saying good things about what he is about to read. He will quietly prepare his opponent for a sort of "Père François"[62] — a very good Father.

I would advise you not to read aloud a text in a language the listener does not know. It is not good taste, and the effect is nil.

After a bit of practice with a single listener, one can try reading aloud to a more numerous audience. If you are gifted, you will rapidly manage to make yourself heard by several thousand listeners: it is just a question of volume — the volume of your voice, I mean.

BAD EXAMPLES[63]

The cabaret, which is in no need of acquiring a bad reputation, has played — and still plays — a quite important role in Artistic and Literary life. Alas! We have quite a few intellectuals just now who do not mind being seen in cafés — at the least — or indeed sitting in full view (often on the terrace), forgetting all the caution a respectable man owes to himself — and even in some ways to other people. Are not this sad aperitif exhibitionism, these public bacchanalia, these intemperate horrors an affront to Morality?

Of course, I have been known to go to a Brasserie; but then, I hide away — not out of blameworthy hypocrisy, but because prudence lends me a certain reserve — and most of all, so as not to be seen. I should be ashamed to be seen! As Alphonse Allais[64] used to tell me: "You could spoil a chance of marriage."

In earlier days, I went from time to time to the Chat noir — as did Maurice Donnay,[65] I may say; and I was often to be found at the Auberge du Clou — but secretly, of course, and I only went there between my meals, which I ate in another tavern, round the corner.

Which shows I am not a café man; I prefer Brasseries. Yes.

In the old days, cafés were very different from now: they were more like cabarets; and the drinks had nothing to do with what is sold these days in bars, bistros, "tea-rooms" or the other places one can find when walking around town. Even so, people drank "seriously," very "seriously"; and one of my great-uncles[66] — who was for many years lieutenant of the Pertuisaniers — recounts in his "ancient memoirs" that he often sank "manye cuppes" with Rabelais[67] at the Pine Cone, the famous cabaret located at the corner of the Rue Copeau and the Contrescarpe Saint-Marcel, outside the Porte Bordet (the Rue Copeau was re-named Rue Lacépède in 1853).

What a fine cabaret! Villon[68] came to the Pine Cone long before Rabelais became a regular along with Despériers, Dolet, Marot,[69] and my uncle.

My uncle, like every good soldier, drank surprising quantities while reeling off a flood of stories whose spiciness made his throat itch and caused him to lift his elbow without stopping. It is annoying that he never knew Villon; the latter would have had quite an earful, though I am the one to say it.

Unfortunately, Villon had "gone dead" some time before — and gave no more thought to drinking, even little sips; anyway, my uncle was only born after Villon's death. Which are all pressing reasons that kept them far apart from each other. Yes.

Those were strange times, when poets could lead such a dubious kind of life without losing their talent or their dignity. Religious writers in later centuries were not often seen in cabarets. Bossuet and Massillon[70] seem to have kept away from such places. They were most likely right in that course of action. Their work would probably have suffered had they gone there, and their renown would surely only have been tarnished. Yes.

Boileau, Racine, Furetière, La Fontaine, Chapelle,[71] Mauvillain the attorney, Brillac the councillor, and other fine minds used to meet in the Golden Bottle on the Place du Cimetière Saint-Jean (currently the site of the Lobau barracks). It was in this cabaret that Racine wrote *Les Plaideurs*. It is hard to believe, isn't it?

These days, Raoul Ponchon[72] knows what going to cafés means. I have often seen him there; on the other hand, he never saw me: I was too well hidden.

I cannot list here all the names I know that go to cafés, you will understand. I don't believe that going to a café, or other places of the sort, is a bad thing in itself; I admit I have worked there a lot; and I do not think the famous people who went there before me were wasting their time. An exchange of ideas takes place there which can only be of value — on condition you do not attract attention.

However, to show my moral concern, and look respectable, I say: "Young people, do not go to cafés; listen to the serious words of a man who has spent too much time there." — but does not regret it for a moment, the monster!

GOOD UPBRINGING[73]

The members of the Académie all had a good upbringing; they are all nice and polite.

In prehistoric times innovators were certainly looked upon no better than they are today.

Alphonse Karr[74] has described the difficulties encountered... in the old days, the very old days... by a primitive scientist, who dared to count up to twenty, using toes as well as fingers. Just think:... a revolutionary!

Imagine the problems to be overcome by the first man to go down a staircase! His friends inevitably made fun of him,... and laughed till they split their sides... he was a "shocker."

And the general surprise that greeted the first Lady to wear a necklace of calves' heads... What a cheek!...

On the other hand, there is reason to believe that the first pot of jam was mysteriously discovered by a child. His parents only learned of the event once the pot was empty — of course.

— "Children are not children any more," they said.

Children like new things. It is only at the age of "reason" that they lose their taste for novelty. They have an instinctive hatred of "old ideas": they guess that they are the ones that will be a "drag" in the future — when they take possession of all their "intelligence" tiny children observe Man, and they "know" him. You can be sure it does not take them long to see what a "dummy" they are looking at.

"What a dunce," they say to themselves.

But that does not last, fortunately!

Man — the animals' superior brother — is the natural instructor of the Child. He is the one who teaches his young pupil how to behave properly at table, in Society, and on the Turf; he also gives the child all the "tricks" needed to get by in earthly and heavenly Life — each "trick" being more honest than the last — for Man, whom we are talking about, is honourableness personified, of course, even if he is a villain... ...consciously or unconsciously.

That is how we were all brought up (very well). The Man of Music, the Man of Letters, the Man of Justice (and their fellows) taught us to think like them, to see like them, to hear like them. They are our moral — or even immoral "fathers." The role of Mother (wife of the Man) is very hidden. For the Man, she remains the Permanent Child.

Curiously, the Mother is not asked for her opinion on the upbringing her children should receive. The Man is the sole master; he decides, magisterially, superiorly, luminously. We must remember that the Man will always be father — Reverend Father — Paternity.

Ladies may take views — and take sides: but they will never be paternal. Just a few days ago, I said to a young mother I was congratulating: — "Of course, maternity is a lovely thing, but what will you say when you are a grandmother?... It is much finer!"

Isn't that a consoling thought?

116

IGOR STRAWINSKY[75]

I have often said — & I shall continue to repeat it long after I am dead — that there is no Truth in Art (no single Truth, I mean).

The Truth of Chopin, that prodigious creator, is not the same as Mozart's, that luxuriant musician whose *writing* is eternally dazzling; just as Gluck's Truth is not the same as Pergolesi's; any more than Liszt's is the same as Haydn's — which is really just as well.

If there is an artistic Truth, where does it begin? Which is the Master who is wholly in possession of it? Is it Palestrina? Is it Bach? Is it Wagner?

To maintain that there is one Truth in Art seems as strange to me, as crazy, as if I heard someone declare the existence of Locomotive-Truth, or House-Truth, Aeroplane-Truth, Emperor-Truth, or Beggar-Truth, etc.; & no one would dream of propounding such an idea — at least not publicly — (out of modesty, perhaps, or plain common sense) for a "type," even if *genuine, real,* must not be confused with Truth.

And yet, Critics specialising in the various Arts are rather inclined to present the public with Idea-Truths which they defend with the full weight of their sumptuous knowledge & authorised competence.

They do it with no fixed purpose, I feel sure, but they do it just the same — & have done for several centuries, the fine fellows (replacing each other along the way, of course): — a habit, presumably.

Would these Gentlemen allow me amicably to differ from their opinion? Would they concede that I have the right not to share their conviction about this matter?

This is why I will never cease repeating, day & night: "There is no Truth in Art."

My illustrious friend Igor Strawinsky — about whom I am going to speak — is living proof of this: he is also the most precise, the most real, the most right example of it.

Igor Strawinsky was born in Oranienbaum — near Petrograd — on 5th (18th)[76] June 1882. His father was an Opera singer in the chorus at the Théâtre Marie & though he guessed the musical gifts his son possessed, he destined him for one of the various mysterious duties to which the study of Law leads.

Dear Strawinsky came very close to being a judge! — or something of that sort. Yes.

Luckily at the age of twenty two, Igor Strawinsky met Rimsky-Korsakov, who was struck by the gifts he could glimpse in this young man, wished to make him his pupil, & snatched him from his studies of human, inhuman, or even superhuman Laws.

This action makes me like Rimsky very much & helps me a little to forget the "misdeeds" of which the author of *Scheherazade* was guilty towards Mussorgsky, (see also the unimaginable "corrections"(?) he made to the score of *Boris Godunov.* The dear man was very "academic"). I must say Strawinsky has very fond memories of his Master, and always speaks of him with great affection, and filial gratitude.

Very quickly — almost immediately — Igor Strawinsky showed who he was and made clear he was worthy of the lessons given by good old Rimsky — who was not mean-spirited, in spite of his pedantic fussiness.

And here I give you a list from which you can see the range of my glorious friend's works: *Symphony in E flat* (1905-07); *The Beast and the Shepherdess*, suite for voice and orchestra (1907); *Fantastic Scherzo*, for orchestra (1907-8); *Fireworks*, for orchestra (1908); *Funeral Chant for the death of Rimsky-Korsakov* (1908); *Four Studies for Piano* (1908); *Two Melodies* (Gorodetzky, 1908); *The Firebird*, story for dance (1909-10); *The "Firebird" Suite* for orchestra; *The "Firebird" Lullaby*, for small orchestra; *Lullaby & Finale* from the *"Firebird"* for small orchestra; *Two Melodies* (Verlaine, 1910); *Petruschka*, burlesques in 4 tableaux (1910-11); *"Petruschka" Suite* for orchestra; *Two Melodies* (Balmont, 1911); *The King of the Stars* (Balmont, male chorus with orchestra, 1911); *The Rite of Spring*, scenes from pagan Russia (1911-13); *Three Melodies from Japanese Poetry*, for female voice & nine instruments (woodwind, piano & strings, 1912); *Childhood Memories*, three childish melodies for vice and piano (1913); *The Nightingale*, opera in 3 acts (1909-14); *The Nightingale's Song*, symphonic poem taken from the second & third acts of the opera *The Nightingale* (1917); *Three Easy Pieces*, for piano duet (easy left hand, 1915); *Five Easy Pieces*, for paino duet (easy right hand, 1917); *The Cat's Lullabies*, suite of songs for female voice & three clarinets (French version by C.-F. Ramuz, 1915-16); *Pribaoutki*, pleasant songs for voice & eight instruments (French version by C.-F. Ramuz, 1914); *Fox*, one act burlesque, for four male voices & orchestra (French version by C.-F. Ramuz, 1916-17); *Study for Pianola* (1917); *Three Childrens' Stories*, songs with piano solo (1917); *Russian Songs*, songs with piano solo (1917); *Village Weddings*, Russian scenes in two parts with songs & music (French version by C.-F. Ramuz, 1917); *Mavra*, an operatic work recently performed at the Opéra de Paris by the "Ballets Russes."

I would like now to present the spirit and character of his work, of which I have given you a summary, with all its verve. But I must loyally announce to you that I will not indulge in any criticism, but will content myself with giving you a sort of description of the splendid, magical talent deployed in these works.

One characteristic of Strawinsky's music is its sonorous "transparency." This is the quality one always finds in the pure Masters, who never leave "residues" in their Sonority — residues that you will always find in the "musical matter" of the Impressionist composers, & even, alas! in that of some Romantic musicians.

Palestrina makes us "hear" this sonorous "transparency"; he had a very high degree of mastery in handling it, & seems to have been the first one to bring this phenomenon into Music.

The exquisite Mozart used it to such effect that one cannot conceive how he managed it. Such mastery leaves one perplexed, before such subtle "clairvoyance" of sound, such a calm and perfect phonic lucidity.

If you listen to any of Igor Strawinsky's works, you will inevitably be struck by the remarkable clarity with which you feel the vibratory "transparency" I have referred to. *The Rite of Spring* is full of it; & this may be the work that comes most strongly and persuasively to mind — you will be bathed in it prodigiously, considerably impregnated therewith.

Although he knows that Perfection is not of this World, he constantly seeks to capture it, subjugate it.

He is as conscientious as can be, and while he may be meticulous & demanding in the result he expects, he is the first to give carefully-prepared examples to the various performers of his works. To see him in rehearsal is to learn many things, for he knows what he wants, & has a top-class knowledge of the means at his disposal.

He is a master of unparalleled dynamism, and shakes the mass of the public, waking them from their apathy. How adroitly and precisely he plays his "dynamism" — above all, never pedantically, & what colour he gives to this voluntary chaos!

Where Strawinsky shows us the full richness of his musical Power, is in his use of "dissonance." Here he stands revealed & plunges us into a far-ranging intellectual excitement. What a wonderful Magician!

For him, "dissonance" makes "pressure" & with it he "pushes" the aware listener's sensitivity. There is nothing hard about his "dissonance"; it flows out, smoothly, undulating gently, always a useful contribution to its presentation.

His style of orchestration is new & bold. He never does a woolly orchestration; he keeps out of the way of "orchestral holes" & "fog" — which has caused the loss of as many musicians as it has navigators — & steers where he wishes.

Notice how Strawinsky's orchestration comes from deep, well-judged instrumentation. His whole "orchestra" is based on instrumental timbre. I tell you, nothing is left to chance. From where does he derive his sumptuous "Truth"?

One should see him as a remarkable logician, both sure-footed & energetic; he is the only composer writing with such magnificent strength, such certain assurance, such constant will.

I would be letting myself down if I failed to quote you the following passage from the pen of M. Ernest Ansermet[77] (*Revue Musicale*, 21 July 1921): "Strawinsky has never told anyone about the sacrifices he has made to let his music evolve: the sacrifice of musical habits, of oaths of fidelity sworn to forms he once loved, of resting places he had struggled to reach, & easier paths merely glimpsed. He did not achieve this development by deliberate design, but forced it by the pitiless logic of his creative capacity. The outcome of this development is a graft grown on savage stock, but whichever way one looks at it, does this graft not seem justified?"

I love & admire Strawinsky because I also see him as a Liberator. He has done more than anyone to set free contemporary "Musical Thinking" — which had very great need of it, poor thing.

I am pleased to have to recognise this, having suffered so much from Wagnerian oppression — I mean, the oppression of Wagnerians. For in those days, Wagner's genius was miserably worshipped by Mediocrity & Ignorance together, followed by a sheep-like crowd.

You can imagine how difficult it was to be a Wagnerian! — even joking: one only had to say aloud: "Oh, Oh... How lovely!" to be taken for an expert or... an imbecile.

Day after day I saw ridicule heaped upon Franck, who was considered non-existent; Chabrier was misunderstood & found himself called an amateur. The Wagner dictatorship was master of all &

odiously dominated public Taste. An Age of desolation! when the great classics themselves seemed thunderstruck.

For many long years we were subjected to the lot which once befell the so-called "Decadent" poets, at the behest of literary partisans who claimed the inheritance of Victor Hugo & belonged to a Sub-Romanticism of Letters; we drank the bitter draughts, underwent the vexations, tasted all the wretchedness that was the lot of Baudelaire, Verlaine, Mallarmé & others.

Today, something has changed: a joyful sun lights up the depths of our souls...

I do not know what I am, but I do know that the man I have just been talking about is one of the greatest musicians there has ever been.

Let us acclaim the name of Strawinsky!

CLAUDE DEBUSSY[78]

Among the greatest musicians of modern times, Debussy is one of the few whose work has had an influence so astonishingly rapid, & immediately profound.

His arrival in the musical Arena — if I may use the term — was a rather disagreeable event for some, & a very happy one for others. These "others" formed a tiny minority, while the "some" made up a huge mass — as sticky & slimy as one could wish.

As always, the opinion of the "tiny minority" triumphed *(following time-honoured custom)* over the "huge mass" — which itself became stuck in the mud of its own blindness. Poor dear *"Huge mass"*!... once again it had energetically put its foot in it — on principle, wouldn't you say? & out of a sort of stubbornness.

I had the pleasure of watching from a good seat the hatching of the Debussy *"egg."* This was only yesterday & yet to some people it seems already old: the *"egg"* — so magnificently hatched — gave birth, in the opinion of those "some people" to ideas, & principles, whose brightness now seems to be tarnished, & no longer sparkling enough to hold its own against more lively lights... For things are moving fast at the moment.

This hypothesis is not admissible; but do not think that this is intended as a criticism or diminution of Debussy's musical & artistic qualities: — no. — It is only meant to point out the weakening of the moral & intellectual power of a *whole* Era, no less; & no specific person is meant to be the target.

Just as Debussy did not make Wagner disappear from Universal Memory, no musician will ever wipe away the name of the composer of *Pelléas & Mélisande*, which glory has engraved for ever in the splendid & very rich Gallery of Musical Honours.

The appearance of a new Genius on this Earth is always the occasion of never-ending "scenes" —

which are merely endless *"drivel"* poured forth about him. It is enough to make you clasp your head in your hands!... The poor "arrival" is immediately seen as an Antichrist, Exterminator, or Raging Madman & scarcely dares even briefly to leave his own home. In short, he is made to see most firmly that he is not welcome, & must simply remain silent. Yes.

Of course in the days of our dear old sadly missed *"grandparents"* in the Stone Age, newly arrived Geniuses were no better received than ours are in the present day, & it was not rare for them to be welcomed with a good stab from a flint dagger between the shoulder blades... Is this not a strange way to thank the Lord for his gracious "dispatch"? Say what you will: it is pretty stiff, & it is not very nice.

Debussy did not escape these *"special"* hindrances. He had no private money, & life was very hard for him, all the more so as he had no streak of cynicism — or of the anchorite. It is a pure miracle that he was able to write & develop his work; & one cannot but be surprised that he managed to do so.

Debussy was born in St-Germain-en-Laye (Seine-et-Oise) on 22 August 1862, & did all his musical studies at the Conservatoire National in Paris. At that time, this establishment was in the Rue du Faubourg-Poissonnière, where it was originally founded *(late XVIIIth Century)*: a huge, very uncomfortable building & rather ugly to look at — a sort of penitentiary with no redeeming features on the outside — nor on the inside, for that matter.

In 1884 the man who was to compose the *Prélude à l'Après-midi d'un Faune* (1893) won the Prix de Rome, an award which officially put an end to his studies & dispatched him for a stay in the Eternal City. An odd aspect of this which was rather touching as well as unexpected, was that it was thanks to Gounod's kind support that he was chosen for this purely academic crowning — *a first rate certificate of one's schooling & authenticity*, I told him as a friend.

In my humble opinion the effort demanded by possession of this prize was irreparably negative for Debussy & affected the best part of him, like the most corrosive poison. Yes.

For many people — very honourable people, of course — the Prix de Rome for Music carries a prestige which is not accorded to recipients of the same diploma for other artistic categories. In Painting this title has for a long time not only had no importance, but is even a derogatory sign, not in the least commended or sought after. I have even seen people in fits of laughter at the sight of a Prix de Rome for Sculpture, to the latter's great surprise.

Why? This is because the judges who award these prizes are generally so completely inadequate that their judgements are like summonses, or condemnations, sentences as degrading as they are deserved. I must say Debussy did not claim glory from this preposterous title. *L'Enfant Prodigue* was the work with which he competed & won it *(a Paris publisher has had the rather annoying idea of publishing this cantata)*.

But it is not strange to see one so high-minded — who scorned the teaching of Franck & my dear Master d'Indy — place his trust in State teaching? In teaching whose essence is so crude? In teaching which leads to the most odious vulgarity?

Physically, Debussy took after his mother. Numerous photographs have made his appearance well known. He enjoyed natural good health, & it was not till a few years before his death that he suffered attacks of the terrible illness that finally took him from us.

His character was, most of all, charming; & his flashes of bad temper proved purely "explosive," & were not followed by lingering ill-feeling; in any case, he did not hold "his" hastiness against you — a sentiment typical of a naïve selfishness which was not unattractive, I assure you.

From the moment I saw him the first time, I was drawn to him & wished to live constantly at his side. For thirty years I had the good fortune to be able to fulfil my wish. We understood one another implicitly, without complicated explanations, for we had known each other — for ever, it seemed.

I knew him through his whole creative development. The *Quartet*, the *Chansons de Bilitis*, *Pelléas & Mélisande*, took shape before my eyes; & I still cannot forget the emotion this music caused me; for I savoured with delight its *"cloudiness,"* precious & new at that time.

And the magnificent piano-pieces struck fairy-like poses at his finger-tips, languished & murmured with tender sadness.

There was a great sureness about him, too great to my mind. It hampered his *"mobility"* & the *"diversity"* of his *"points of view."* I suffered to see him so.

Have you read *Consuelo*?[79] Haydn's devoted admiration for Porpora suggested to me a similar devotion to my great companion.

I also liked to hear him play Chopin — a composer he was very fond of. No-one played him better than he: he could analyse & understand him as few virtuosi have shown themselves able to do.

My poor friend! To think that if he was still alive today we would now be the worst of enemies. Life — & the *"debussystes"* — would have ensured we were separated & torn hatefully apart: we no longer followed the same path; our horizons were diverging by the hour. So what then?...

Our long intimacy was to be disrupted by this forever.

Freedom of thought will never be of this World, alas! If absolutely necessary, I understand quite easily that one can have a preference, even a marked preference, for one's own ideas — one's very own, personal ideas — & that other people's may seem defective & generally uninteresting, deserving to be stifled. This way of seeing things is too human for me to find any substantial cause for reproach; it is self-explanatory & is in itself a thought, which, though it is brutal & discourteous, has a right to general respect. That is how partisan people proceed — & without being troubled by it, either. Yes.

And yet, how can we accept, without nodding our head in every direction, that serious intellectuals can use this convenient but inelegant stratagem? I ask myself softly — with the soft pedal.

Yet that is what we see every day — or at least every other day. So I say: Is man — our fellow-creature — insatiable, poor thing?... vain?... ferocious?... Humph!

I would like to discuss one point which served as a pretext for controversy between different critics: the theory of *"debussysme."*

Debussy's aesthetics are attached to symbolism in several of his works; they are impressionist in his work as a whole. Please forgive me, am I not to some extent the cause of this? So it is said.

This is the explanation:

When I met him, at the start of our friendship, he was completely impregnated with Mussorgsky & was conscientiously searching for a way forward which was not easy to find. On that count I had a long lead over him; I was not weighed down with "prizes" of Rome or any other town, given that I do not carry such prizes either on my person or on my back; for I am a man in the manner of Adam (*he of Paradise*), who never carried off a prize — doubtless he was a lazy man.

I was at that time writing *The Son of the Stars* — to a text by Joséphin Péladan; & I explained to Debussy the need for us French to prize ourselves away from the Wagnerian adventure, which did not correspond to our natural aspirations, & I explained to him that I was by no means anti-Wagnerian, but that we needed to have our own music — with no sauerkraut if possible.

Why not use the means of representation exhibited to us by Claude Monet, Cézanne, Toulouse-Lautrec, etc.? Why not transpose these means into music? Nothing could be simpler. Are they not expression?

This was the point of departure for experiments which were fertile in almost-certain results — fruitful, even... Who could show him examples? reveal finds to him? suggest which piece of ground to dig in? provide him with carefully weighed observations?... Who?...

I do not wish to answer: it no longer interests me.

Dying generations inexorably lose their "living" action. They take on other virtues; but since the death of our dear Prehistoric grandparents — of whom I spoke a short while ago — the human mind has not changed; it is still to be found in the same place as when it started out down here: ...in the skulls of men — & women.

Erik SATIE

......

...... L'élève doit avoir beaucoup de patience — — une grande patience —

— une patience de cheval ,... très grosse ......

... Car il est utile... qu'il s'habitue... à supporter son professeur ....

......

Pensez donc : .... un professeur ! ...
il pose des questions qu'il sait ,.. lui,
... & que vous ne savez pas ,.... vous...

Il abuse ,.... évidemment ....

......

Et vous avez le droit de ne rien dire ...
...... C'est même mieux .....
....
......
......
......

Manuscript for the talk Child Musicians *(excerpt).*

A EULOGY OF CRITICS[80]

Ladies,
> Young Ladies,
>> Gentlemen

─────

It is not chance that made me choose this subject:
> "A Eulogy of Critics" —

It is gratitude, ... for I am as grateful as I am gracious . . . .
Last year, I gave several lectures on "Intelligence & Musicality among Animals" . . .
Today I shall speak about "Intelligence & Musicality among Critics" . . . .
It is more or less the same theme, with modifications, of course.

> . . . .

> . . . .

Friends have told me this is a thankless subject, ... Why should it be thankless? . . . . . There is no lack of thanks involved in it; at least I cannot see that is the case; . . . . I will go ahead & speak in praise of critics . . . .

> . . . .

> . . . .

> . . . .

> . . . .

Critics are not known as well as they should be; people do not know what they have done, what they are capable of. . . . .
In short. . . , they are as misunderstood as the animals, though like them, they have a certain usefulness.

> . . . .

> . . . .

Yes . . . . They are not only the creators of the Art of criticism, that Master of all the Arts, they are the leading thinkers of the world, the free thinkers of the social scene, I venture to say. . . . . .

> . . . .

> . . . .

> . . . .

> . . . .

In fact, it was a critic who posed for Rodin's "Thinker." . . . .
. . . . . I learned this information from a critic, a fortnight ago, or three weeks at the most . . . .
. . . . & it gave me pleasure, great pleasure . . . . .

. . . . Rodin had a weakness for critics, a great weakness . . . . .Their advice was dear to him — very dear — too dear, priceless.

. . . .

. . . .

There are three sorts of critic:. . . . . those of importance; . . . . . those with less of it; . . . . .
— those with none at all . . . .

. . . .

The latter two sorts do not exist —
— all critics . . . . are of *importance* . . . .

. . . .

. . . .

. . . .

. . . .

Physically the critic looks grave & deep, ...
they are the double-bassoon type. . . . .
They are a centre in themselves, — a centre of gravity . . .
If they laugh, — they laugh only with one eye, —
— either the good one, ... — or the bad one. . . . . They are always very sweet to the
Ladies— but keep the Gentlemen at a distance,
— calmly. . . . .

. . . .

. . . .

In short, — they are rather intimidating, — though very nice to look at, ...
They are serious men, ... as serious as a Buddha, a *boudin noir*,[81] of course.

. . . .

. . . .

Mediocrity, or incompetence are not to be found among critics . . . .
A mediocre
— or incompetent —
critic would be the laughing stock of his colleagues;
— it would be impossible for him to practise his profession, — or rather, his calling, — for he
would have to leave his country —
— even his birthplace; — & every door would be closed to him; —
— his life would be nothing but a long torture — of terrible monotony.

. . . .

. . . .

The Artist is but a dreamer,—
— when it comes down to it; — . . . . . .
. . . . the critic, — however, — has the conscience of reality, —
— & his own, — as well. —

— An artist can be imitated, — a critic is inimitable, — & priceless . . . .

. . . . How would one imitate a critic? —

— I wonder —

Besides, — it would be of slender, very slender, interest;

. . . . We have the original, ... *that is enough for us* . . . .

. . . . . The person who said criticism was plain sailing did not say anything very remarkable.

— He should even be ashamed to have said it;

— he should be prosecuted, or pursued, — at least for a mile —

— or two.

— Will the man who wrote such a thing . . . . . .

. . . . . . perhaps live to regret his remark? —

— It is possible, ... it is to be hoped, ... *it is certain* . . . . . .

. . . .

. . . .

A critic's brain is a store, —

— a department store.

. . . .

You can find anything there: — orthopaedics, — sciences, — bed-linen, — arts, —travelling rugs, — a wide range of furniture, — French & foreign writing paper; —

— smoker's wares,

gloves, — umbrellas, —

— woollens, — hats, — sports, — walking sticks, — optician's, — perfumery, — et cetera.

The critic knows everything, — . . . . sees everything, — hears everything, — touches everything, . . .

moves everything around . . . . . , eats anything . . . . . , confuses everything . . . . — & thinks nothing of it . . . .

What a man!! . . . .

Tell the world!!! . . . .

All our wares are guaranteed!!! . . . .

In hot weather, —

the merchandise is kept inside!!!

Inside the critic!! . . . . . .

Look!!

. . . . . . Take note, but do not touch!!!

It is unique!!!! . . .   Unbelievable!!!

. . . .

. . . .

The critic is also a crow's nest, ... —

— a buoy, — I may add. . . . . which marks the reefs that run along the shores of the Human

Spirit. . . . . .

. . . . . . Near to these shores, —
these false-shores,

— the Critic stands guard, —
— proud in his perceptiveness . . . . ,
— from afar, — he looks a little like a boundary post, —
— but a friendly post, —
— intelligent.

. . . .

. . . .

How do they reach this high position,—
this position as buoy, — or boundary post?

. . . .

By merit, —

— by personal, agricultural merit[82] . . . . . . I say "Agricultural" because
they cultivate the love of the Just & the Beautiful . . . . . .

. . . .

. . . .

This brings us on to a delicate point . . . . . .

. . . .

Critics are recruited by choice, —
like those products referred to as "choice," —

— extra-superior,

— top quality . . . . .

. . . . . . The Editor of a newspaper, a review, — or any other periodical, — is the one who finds the critic
he needs to complete his editorial team . . . . . . *No recommendation can make any difference* . . . . .

. . . . . . He finds him as the result — of a severe examination of his conscience . . . . . — . . . . . This
examination is very long and painful, — both for the critic and the Editor.

. . . . . . One asks questions; the other has doubts . . . .

. . . . . It is an agonising struggle full of surprises . . . . .

. . . . All kinds of subterfuge are used by both sides . . . . . . In the end, the Editor is defeated. . . .

. . . . This is what generally happens, if the critic is thoroughbred and has been carefully trained

. . . . . .

The Editor is absorbed, and gradually reduced by the critic . . . .

It is rare for the Editor to escape . . . .

. . . .

. . . .

. . . .

. . . .

Real critical sense does not consist of criticising oneself, but other people; —
— & the beam in one's own eye does nothing to stop one seeing the mote in one's neighbour's eye; —
— in this case, the beam becomes a telescope, — a long telescope . . . .
which magnifies the mote out of all proportion.

· · · · · · · · · ·

· · · · · · · · · ·

One could hardly admire too much the courage of the first critic to introduce himself to the world . . . .
· · · · · · · · · · The rude inhabitants of the Ancient Night of Time must have greeted him with heavy kicks to the belly, not realising he was a precursor worthy of veneration . . . . . .
· · · · · · · · · . In his own way, he was a hero.

· · · · · · · · · ·

· · · · · · · · · ·

The second, third, fourth and fifth critics were certainly no better received, . . . but helped to create a precedent: —

· · · · · · · · · ·

the Art of criticism gave birth to itself. It was its first New Year's day . . . . .
A long time after, these Benefactors of Humanity learned to organise themselves better.— They formed Critic's Unions in all the major capitals, —

· · · · · · · · · ·

Critics therefore became important personalities, —
— which goes to show that virtue is always rewarded . . . .
Suddenly, — artists were put in harness, ... made to submit like tabby-cats . . . . . .

· · · · · · · · · ·

· · · · · · · · · ·

It is right that Artists should be guided by critics. —
I have never understood Artists' touchiness about critics' pronouncements. . . . .
. . . . . I think there is an element of pride in this, —
misplaced pride, —
— which is not pleasing . . . . .
. . . . . Artists would gain by venerating critics a little more; by listening to them with respect; by liking them even, and inviting them often to family meals, — to sit between Uncle and Grandpa . . . .
· · · · · · · · · ·
. . . . They should follow my example, —
— my good example: —
— I am dazzled by the presence of a critic, he shines so brightly that I blink for more than an hour afterwards, —
— I kiss the footprints of his slippers: —

— I drink in his words from a big stemmed glass, out of politeness . . . .

. . . .

. . . .

. . I have studied a great deal the behaviour of Animals . . . .

. . . .

— Alas! — they have no critics; . . .

. . . .

— This Art is foreign to them; —

— at least, I know no work of the kind in the archives of my Animals . . . . . .

. . . .

— Perhaps, — my critic friends know of one, —

or several . . . . .

Would they be kind enough to tell me, — the sooner the better? . . . . .

. . . .

. . . .

Yes, animals have no critics. . . . .

. . . .

. . .The wolf does not criticise the sheep: . . .

. . . . . it eats it; —

— not that it despises the sheep's art, —

— but because it admires the flesh, and even the bones — of this woolly animal . . . . . which is so good, ... so good in a stew. . . .

. . . .

. . . .

. . . .

I notice it is getting late . . . .

. . . . I shall have to end my eulogy at this point . . . . .

. . . . . It is a subject I shall return to

— later, —

— another time . . . . .

. . . .

. . . .

. . . . . . Today, — I will close this talk by saying this: —

. . . .

. . . .

We need a discipline — of iron, —

— or some other metal . . . .

. . . .

. . . . Only critics — can impose it, —

— can ensure it is maintained, —
     — from afar . . . . . .

        . . . .

They ask only to inculcate in us the excellent principle of obedience . . . .
      . . . . . . He who disobeys is to be pitied; . . . . . for not to obey is very sad . . . . . But one must not obey one's evil passions, ... even if they themselves tell us to . . . . How can one tell whether passions are evil?. . . . . . evil as the eye?. . . . .
     Yes, — how? . . . . . By the pleasure one has in yielding to them,
     . . . . . giving oneself up to them, ... *and because critics do not like them* . . . . . . They have no evil passions . . . . How could the fine fellows have them?
     . . . . . .They have no passions at all — *none* . . . . They are always calm, and think only of their duty: . . . . . to correct the poor world's failings, ... and make a decent living from it, ... so they can buy themselves tobacco, — quite simply. . . . .

         . . . .
      . . . . . . That is their task, ...
        . . . . . . the task incumbent upon these men of good counsel; . . . . .
      . . . . . . for where they have one they have a thousand —
     — counsels —
        — municipal councils. . . . .

         . . . .

           . . . .

          . . . .

      . . . . . . Let us thank them for the sacrifices they make daily for our good, —
     — for our sole good; —
— let us ask Providence to protect them against illness of all kinds; —
     — to keep them from all kinds of annoyance; —
— to grant them a great number of children of every species — which might continue theirs . . . .

      . . . . These wishes can do them neither good —
     — nor ill.

        . . . .

        . . . .

          . . . .

. . . . But at least —
     — it will give them quite a pile —
        — to write about.

CHILD MUSICIANS[83]

Ladies,

      Young Ladies,

            Gentlemen, . . .

. . . Last year, . . . I had the honour of giving, . . here, . . . a talk on "Music & Animals" . . . I had written an article in the *Revue Musicale S.I.M.* on *Intelligence and Musicality Among Animals* . . .

. . . . Today, . . . I am going to talk about "Child Musicians" . . This title may be too broad, . . . too all-embracing . . . I know. . .

. . . What follows is more like advice, . . . suggestions . . . addressed to my charming young audience . . .

. . . .

Would grown-ups please excuse me if I shorten this talk in this way. . . though the tone, . . . I may say, . . . will be quite friendly. . . & with no pretensions . . .

. . . .

. . . .

. . . .

. . . . I have lived for a long time . . . with animals; . . . . and I have. . . spent a lot of time . . . with children . . .

. . . Myself, I was once, . . . a child — *though you would not think so* — a tiny child, . . . tiny, . . . you still see them these days; . . . . .I was . . . no smaller, . . . and no bigger. . . than these ones, — of course. .

. . . .

I have continued . . . to have a soft spot . . . for animals . . . There are many that I love very much: . . . . . . lobster, . . . for instance; . . . but it gives me a stomach ache, . . . unfortunately for it, . . . otherwise, . . . I would eat it more often . . . .

. . . .

As far as children are concerned, . . . their musical aspirations . . . can be set out as follows: . . . those that like music; . . . . . . those it does not bother too much; . . . & those that find it altogether, . . . incurably, . . . ferociously. . . annoying.

. . . .

. . . .

For the last ones. . . I have no hard feelings . . .

. . . . After all, . . . they are strictly within their rights . . .

. . . . So, ... I who am speaking, . . . I do not like veal: . . .

. . . I find it too cold, . . . even in the height of summer, . . . in a heat wave. . .

. . . . It is one of the few animals. . . I dislike . . . except the head, . . . which is very good in oil. . .

. . . .

Chacun son goût, . . isn't it?. . .

. . . I think I am right, . . .
   completely right,
      perfectly right,
         righter than right . . .

         . . . .
  no beating about the bush: . . .
       . . . . *I tell myself so quite frankly* . . .

       . . . .

          . . . .
  Besides, . . . I am always right . . .

. . . .

    . . . .

       . . . .
  . . . . . How does one become a musician? . . . . . .
It is quite simple: . . . . .
       . . . one finds a teacher —
— a music teacher, . . . if possible. . .
. . . .
  One chooses him carefully, . . .
  attentively, ...
        severely. . .
      . . .
      One agrees a price . . .

. . . . .

. . . .

  At this point, . . I prefer to tell you . . . one should not get carried away:
. . . an hour . . . is quickly up . . .
   . . . yes, . . . one agrees a price, . . but. . . a good price. . . for oneself
    — *moderate* . . . . . Yes. . .

. . . .
I do not know. . . . if I make myself clear[84]

       . . . .

       . . . .

. . . .
      Next one must buy a metronome . . . .
Above all, . . . one that is not too ripe . . .
   . . . .
   . . . . Nice and plump, . . .
. . . .

a little fat . . .

. . . .

. . . .
. . . . One that works properly . . . There are metronomes. . .
that work out of time, . . . like madmen . . .
. . . . There are even ones . . . that do not work at all . . .
. . . *They are not good metronomes* . . .

. . . .

. . . .
. . . Next . . . I would advise you . . . to buy. . . a music-stand . . .
. . . They come at all prices . . .
. . . .
. . . . *You will be spoilt for choice.*
. . . .
. . . .

. . . .

. . . .
The pupil must have a lot of patience —
— great patience —
— *the patience of a horse,* . . . a big one . . .
. . . For it is useful . . . to get used . . .
to putting up with the teacher.
. . . .

. . . .
Just think, now: . . . a teacher! . . . .
he asks things he knows, . . . already, . . .
& which you do not know, ...
. . . .
Obviously, ... he is taking advantage. . . . .

. . . .
. . . .
And you have a right to say nothing . . .
. . . .
. . . . . *It may even be better* . . . .
. . . .
. . . .
. . . .
. . . .
. . . .

Do not take revenge on your instrument . . .

. . . .

Instruments are often subjected . . .
to pretty rough treatment . . .

They get beaten . . .

. . . .

. . . . .

I have known children who took pleasure . . .
in treading on the feet of their pianos . . .
. . . . . Others . . . who do not put their violin . . . . back in its box . . . . So, ... the poor creature . . .
catches cold . . . . . & gets ill . . . .
. . . . . *That is not nice* . . . No . . . .

. . . .

. . . .

. . . . . . Some of them . . . . put snuff . . .
in their trombone —
which is very unpleasant . . . . for the instrument . . . .
When they blow, . . . they fling this itchy dust . . . in the face . . . of their neighbour, . . . who sneezes &
coughs . . . for more than half an hour . . . . .

. . . .

Peuf! . . .

. . . .

The consequences are serious. . . Afterwards, . . .
the instrument does not work properly . . . & has to be repaired . . .

. . . .

These are very regrettable things, . . . very painful, . . . very sad —
— which cause me much pain. . .

. . . .

. . . .

. . . .

. . . .

. . . .

. . . .

Practice must be done in the morning, . . . after breakfast . . . .
You must be very clean . . . .
Have blown your nose . . . .

. . . .

. . . . . Do not start work with jammy fingers . . .

. . . .

. . . .

. . . .

And you must not break off — every five minutes — to go and fetch sweets, . . . nougat, . . . barley sugar, . . . biscuits, . . . chocolate, . . .

. . or other things like that . . . .

. . . .

. . . .

. . . .

The times . . . . & days for the lesssons . . . are fixed with the agreement of the pupil . . . . & the teacher . . .

. . . . It would be rather inconvenient . . . if the pupil . . . had his lesson at one time — & on one day — while the teacher . . . . gave his at a different time — & day.

. . . .

That often happens in the Faculties: . . .

. . . there are students . . . who never see their teachers . . .

. . . .

A curious application . . . of the facultative

. . . .

. . . .

. . . .

Do not follow this procedure . . . .

. . . .

Since, . . . you must necessarily . . . be in tune . . .

. . . . . .

The pupil . . . & the teacher . . . came into the World . . .

to meet each other, . . . at least from time to time.

. . . .

Otherwise, . . .

where would we be? . . . . Yes, . . where would we be? . . .

. . . .

I shall tell you: . . . . .

. . . . we would be going . . . nowhere . . .

. . . .

. . . .

. . . .

. . . .

You must know that work . . . is freedom . . .

— . . . freedom . . . for other people . . .

While you are working, ... you are not bothering anyone . . .

136

Do not forget that . . . .
You understand? . . . . Sit down . . . .
. . . .

. . . .

. . . .

. . . .

. . . .

. . . . I have to . . . bring this talk to an end,
. . . . . time is getting on . . .
. . . .

. . . . It will soon . . . be six o'clock in the evening . . .
I am going to have my tea, ...
then, . . . I shall go for a walk —
— to work up an appetite . . . .
. . . .

. . . .

. . . .

Be good, . . . children . . .
. . . .

. . . .

Thank you for listening . . .
. . . . & . . . greetings . . . from your old friend . . .
. . . .

. . . .

. . . .

. . . .

. . . .

. . . .

. . . .

It remains only to thank . . . the grown-ups —
— who were good enough to listen to me . . .
. . . .

Kindly allow me . . . your humble servant . . .

. . . . . to offer my . . . sincerest regards

MUSICAL SPIRIT[85]

Ladies,
      Young Ladies,
           Gentlemen —

I am here to speak to you about Music — a pretty vast topic for one talk — So I shall greatly restrict my subject, and simply speak a little about musicians, &, especially, about musical Spirit.

    Musicians are recruited from every background; . . .they come from all social classes . . .

    . . . Musical teaching is done in the same way as all teaching; . . . it is given by masters, . . . & received by pupils — WHO ARE MORE OR LESS GOOD — (AS ARE THE MASTERS, LIKEWISE. . .).

    . . .After several years, the pupil becomes what is commonly known as an *"artist"* & is launched into the World . . . & through it . . .

    So far, . . . so good . . .

. . . .

    In fact, . . . what does this . . . new arrival . . . know?
He knows: . . .

    Harmony . . .
          Counterpoint . . .
                Instrumentation . . .
                Orchestration . . .
    . . . . Melody holds no secrets for him, . . . any more than does Rhythm;
Pitch . . .
          Dynamics . . .
                Tone (& the ATONAL SYSTEM) . . .

. . . .

    He cultivates Wisdom . . . He is imaginative . . .

    He has a touch of self-denial compounded by a most copious . . . enormous, if I may say so — desire for sacrifice . . . His patience is exceptional . . .

    In short, he is ready for the struggle . . . He will fight loyally . . .

    Please remember that all these things are well known to the Critics themselves . . . For the Critics, . . . of course, . . . know everything, . . . & possess every good quality.

    . . . Look at Messieurs Vuillermoz, . . . Laloy, . . . Schloe(t)zer[86]: . . .yes, . . . they know everything! . . .(AT LEAST, . . . I SUPPOSE SO). . .

    . . . Do not, . . . I beg you, . . . take what I am saying in an aggressive sense . . .

    I am merely stating facts . . . which in no way detract from the renown of respectable and respect-worthy Critics — whom I respect . . .

    . . . .

I am too much of a Free-Thinking spirit not to tolerate the thinking of others — even if they present themselves to me as implacable, slightly disloyal adversaries . . . .

. . . . I am neither attacking nor glorifying anyone . . . Today I have even relinquished . . . the irony which is habitual for me . . .

. . . I speak to you as a friend — an old friend, of course . . .

But it is not enough to be a musician — or to look like one — one must have the right spirit . . .

. . . . This is a spirit like any other;

. . . . it is brother to the Literary spirit, . . . to the Pictorial spirit, . . . to the Scientific spirit, . . . & several other spirits — each more spiritual than the last . . .

. . . Only, . . . those that are animated by this spirit can hope to climb up to certain heights of thinking, . . . certain summits of speculation . . .

. . . . Dear friends, I tell you that it is the spirit belonging to each art which gives the artist the necessary courage to endure the violence of the struggles . . .

. . . For in Art, . . . it is all in the struggle, . . . & the struggles are many, . . . repeated, . . . merciless . . .

Above all, . . . one must not compromise . . .

. . . To capitulate will always be a sign of weakness — if not cowardice . . .

. . . .

So we see that most Critics — in Music, as with any Art — do not have the "SPIRIT" of the things they write about . . .

. . . Which is why their point of view so often differs from that of the author they are judging . . .

Please note that I am not questioning their integrity; . . . I only speak, here, about serious Critics; . . . the others do not interest me enough for me to bother with them. . .

I hope they will not therefore see in my words any ill will towards them: . . .

they are not in any way the object of my unfavourable attention . . .

. . . May the Good Lord protect them, . . . bless them, . . . heap them with happiness — if he will be so kind . . .

. . . .

In intellectual matters, there are special conventions about these things.

If one wants to be right — genuinely right — one must start by being reasonable, very reasonable (NOTE THAT THIS IS NOT A PLEONASM); . . .

Besides, . . . one must be right without vanity, . . . or noise, . . . or pride . . . The possession of Right does not grant any privileges; . . .

. . . . often it only causes problems . . .

. . . . The man who is right is — generally — rather badly looked upon . . . even with spectacles . . .

. . . . He should know this, & not have any ambition besides being right — if that is what he is after. . .

. . . . But anyone wishing to preserve their personal tranquillity will take care always to be wrong, . . . completely wrong — or even more . . . .

. . . . .Then, . . . he can be assured of happy days, . . . & he will pass away in honour and prosperity; — &, . . . perhaps he will have many children— legitimate, natural — or supernatural . . .

. . . .

. . . The practice of Art invites us to live in most absolute renunciation . . .

. . . It was not as a joke that I spoke to you, . . . just now, . . . about sacrifice . . .

Music demands a great deal from those that wish to serve it . . . That is what I wished to make you feel . . .

. . . .

A true musician must be at the service of his Art; he must place himself above human miseries; . . . he must draw his courage from within himself, ... himself alone.

CLUBS AND SOCIETIES IN THE COMING FORTNIGHT[87]

NO NEED TO THROW OLD JEWELLERY AWAY. Sell it for a high price. With the proceeds from this fruitful transaction simply buy a share — the lion's — in

the new *Aqueduct Building Society.*

You can apply every Sunday morning from 9 to 11 at Maison Douau, 43 Rue Emile-Raspail.

Contributions: 1 fr. per week. Capital & profits will be shared out every three years.

NO MORE BALDNESS! if everyone makes sure they join the new Aqueduct Building Society.

With your profits you can buy yourself hair lotion.

Maison Douau, 43 rue Emile-Raspail.

IF YOU WISH TO BECOME AS STRONG AS AN OX, and agile as a deer, come to lessons at the "Arcueil-Cachan Young People's Society."

Monsieur L. Cousin will undertake to give you a constitution of first class forged iron.

Not to go is to wish yourself ill.

Go on, get on with it!

The address: Maison Macary.

ATTACKED BY THE APACHES,[88] a local youngster held his own superbly, & caused a great deal of damage to his abominable attackers.

How did he achieve this feat, with such ease? Yes, how?

Because he followed most assiduously the courses in *Physical Development* at the "Arcueil-Cachan Young People's Society." This useful club is run by Monsieur L. Cousin.

Address: Maison Macary, Place de la République (town hall).

DO YOU HAVE BLACK THOUGHTS? A burning sensation in the bottom of your stomach? Quick! Run round to Rue Emile-Raspail, No 60, to "Friendly Jacob's" where the *La Marguerite* dancing classes are held.

You can tell me about it afterwards!

RAGING MAD because he could not go to the magnificent rollicking cinematographic sessions given every Saturday at 8.45pm by Mr Ollinger-Jacob in his superb salon, one unfortunate has been locked up.

Mr Ollinger-Jacob is a philanthropist doubling as a benefactor of suffering Humanity; with well-chosen thermo-cinematographic sessions, he cures the most incurable cases of hypochondria & acute neurasthenia.

Many letters & testimonials.

It is well worth knowing about.

BITTEN BY A MONKEY is not so nice as going to 60 Rue Emile-Raspail — to Friendly Jacob's — where the *La Marguerite* dancing classes are held.

DO NOT FORGET to go every Saturday, at a quarter to nine, to 60 Rue Emile-Raspail.

You will be received by Mr Ollinger-Jacob, the friendly director of the "biggest Cinematograph in the Whole World."

Like a true magician, Mr Ollinger-Jacob will show you every leading brand of spectacle: comedies, high drama, travels, fantasies, artistic films, what do I know! . . .

The price of seats is derisorily cheap.

Families of more than one hundred persons pay a special, proportional price.

A GENTLEMAN offers for free to show all those affected by incommensurable tedium, profound disgust with existence, or unending bitterness, an infallible way to be promptly cheered up, as it did for him after he had suffered & tried in vain all the prescribed pleasures. This offer, whose humanitarian aim will be appreciated, is the result of a vow:

Go every Saturday, at a quarter to nine, to 60 Rue Emile-Raspail, to Mr Ollinger-Jacob's, the eminent director of the Grand Cinematograph.

Make no mistake.

YOU ARE BEING HAD if you do not know that Mr Ollinger-Jacob, celebrated director of the Grand Cinematographic Theatre of the Whole World expects you every Saturday at half-past eight, in the evening of course, at 60 Rue Emile Raspail, in his superb halls. Mr Ollinger-Jacob has been decorated with several fictitious orders of chivalry, he is purveyor by appointment to the Imperial Court of the Sahara, to His Bigness the Doge of Manchester (England), & to His Highness the Sultan of Livarot. A wonderful show, enormous enjoyment. It is always fun!

MUST BE SEEN before you die of boredom, the Grand Jac-Oll Cinema, 60 Rue Emile-Raspail. It is unbelievable! Go there once, & you'll be going back forever. Mr Ollinger-Jacob — or Jacob-Ollinger — who has the gift of unrivalled graciousness, is available to look after the audience's comfort every day.

Wonderful grand show on Saturdays at nine.

MR OLLINGER-JACOB, the famous director of the Grand "Oll-Jac" cinematograph, is coolly continuing his series of unique presentations. People are being turned away!

New show every Saturday.

III. PRIVATE WRITINGS

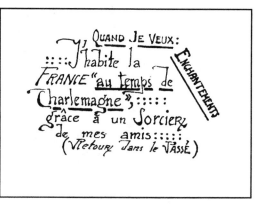

····· en rentrant chez
moi, j'y trouvai un riche
trousseau ; ... & un somptueux
mobilier remplaçait l'ancien.
···· Sur une table, je
vis un carnet de chèques
inépuisable ···· Un vieux
domestique se tenait à
mes ordres ···

Un trousseau féerique ;
un mobilier princier ;
un carnet de chèque inépuisable ;
un domestique dévoué ;
l'Art de me rendre invi-
sible , tels sont les
cadeaux que me fit mon
ami le MAGICIEN, pour
m'être agréable ···
Personne ne le sut ····

Man is as much made to dream as I am to have a wooden leg.[89]

I am called Erik Satie like anyone else.

I have always proposed that free cruises should be organised in the ship of State; so far, no one has taken up the idea.

What I would like to see, is all Frenchmen, actually born on French soil, of parents that are French, or at least look it, have a right to a job as a postman in the Paris post office.

Though I am a Catholic, I have never wished to see the number of archbishops in Paris increased to around three hundred.

The more musicians we have, the more madmen we have.

Musicians may be the most modest of animals, but they are also the proudest. It was they who invented the sublime art of ruining poetry.

I do not see why money should have no smell, since it can get anything it wants.

The piano, like money, is only pleasant to those who have the touch.

Gift to the Pope
This gift consists of a splendid beret made of silver, completely lined with mahogany, a salad bowl in alpaca wool, & a pig-schaum pipe.

It is rumoured that a horse has recently had its first communion in a parish near Vienna. This is the first occurrence of this sort of religious phenomenon in Europe; there are references to a jaguar in Australia which acts as a Protestant vicar, & is said to be managing very well. It is true that there is not much to do.

Saint Golin the Arctician
He gave a polar bear its first communion.
As there was no lawyer in the vicinity, Saint Golin had its religious testament stamped & sealed by a penguin.

A villainous hand tiptoed in, with its eyes popping out, & made off with the treasure.

If I am loath to say out loud what I think to myself, it is only because my voice is not strong enough.

You should not let thoughts from the back of your head slide too far down your back.

Man is a heap of bones & flesh.
This heap is run by a contraption called a brain.
The brain sits in what is called the cranial aperture.
The aperture has no apparent opening.
In it, the brain can see nothing, & hear nothing of what is going on around it, as it is isolated from the rest of the World.
This is why Man behaves with the charming lack of conscience so well known to observers, the lack of conscience which characterises him & gives him "personality," if I may say so.

When a man starts talking about the "decadence" we see these days, have a good look at his face.

Drinking absinthe means killing yourself sip by sip.

Musical evolution is always a hundred years behind pictorial evolution.

Joan of Arc was shot by an English firing-squad.

...When I came home, I found a sumptuous wardrobe;... & valuable furniture replacing what I had before.
...On a table I saw an inexhaustible cheque-book... An old man servant stood waiting for my orders...

A magical *trousseau;* princely *furnishings;* an inexhaustible *cheque-book;* a <u>devoted *man-servant;*</u> the Art of making myself invisible; these are the gifts I was given by my friend *the Magician,* to be nice to me...
No one ever knew...

What is man? A poor creature set on this earth to bother other men.

Why is a man good-looking?
Because of all the animals, man is the only one that says so.

They cannot know this; they do not read the paper I read every day.

146

I never read a paper that shares my opinion; it would be distorted.

The horse is an equestrian, domestic, & sporting animal.
    I. Equestrian — a general on its back.
    II. Domestic — a plough attached behind.
    III. Sporting — a rival to beat.

      Training horses is a simple — very simple game... I trained one recently,... an untameable beast... I clamped onto it... my legs: ...It reared. I remained unmoved... & in position... It lay on its back:...I sat on its belly...
      Then it sat down on its backside:... I climbed on its head... So it rolled its head on the ground: I climbed on its rump... In the end, it calmed down, ... reduced to nothing ... it could see I was its master... its good master...

    Hair is no longer a danger
Hair is a parasite which lives on the heads of Men. It takes the form of very long, thin worms.
This parasite is surprisingly voracious & is one of the causes of baldness; by continuous suction it absorbs the capillary juices lying beneath the cranial skin, thus denuding irrevocably the said skin, & bringing about its own death.
In a short space of time Man becomes bald, & is rid of a bothersome, repulsive visitor.
He is cured, & at no risk of the condition returning.

      Truth as told in classroom textbooks

A person who lives in a castle is a...............................	castellan;
A person who lives in a theatre is an	actor;
A person who lives in a prison is a	prisoner;
A person who lives in a boat is	aboater;
A person who lives in an hotel is an	hotelier;
A person who lives in a tower is a	tourist;
A person who lives in an automobile is an	autocrat;
A person who lives in a villa is a	villager;
A person who lives in a boulevard is a......................	boulevardier;
A person who lives in a bank is a	banker;
A person who lives in a passage is a	passenger;
& a person who lives in a tree is a	tre(e)acle tart

      Though our information is false, we do not vouch for it.

Specialist in Funeral marches.
Requiems, Masses arranged for Balls.
The firm will deal with all harmonic repairs.
Rapid transformation of symphonies, quartets, etc. etc.
Serious music made fun.
The most difficult pieces arranged for one finger.
Vocal Melodies arranged for two pianos.
No more incomprehensible compositions.
Subtlety within reach of everyone.
Sonatas reduced, reharmonised.
Our music comes with guaranteed playability.

Attractions

Some Pianos, upright as an *I*, other Grands gaping like every animal in creation. Violins of gummed paper. Drums done up with crocodile skin. Monstrous Harps with a special toboggan for glissandos, oboes ... It is rare to see several players together on the same instrument as happens every day on the piano: there are no duets written for four cheeks on the Oboe, so to speak.

2 Piston Flutes (in F sharp)
1 Alto Overcoat (in C)
1 Spout (in E)
2 Slide Clarinets (in G flat)
1 Syphon (in C)
3 Keyboard Trombones (in D flat)
1 Skin Double Bass (in C)
Chromatic Water-Tub (in B)

Instruments from the wonderful family of Cephalophones, with a range of thirty octaves, completely unplayable. An amateur in Vienna tried, in 1875, to use the Syphon in C; following the execution of a trill, the instrument burst, snapped his spine & completely scalped him. Since then, no one has dared to make use of the powerful resources of the Cephalophones & the State has been obliged to refuse to teach the instruments in local schools.

So when will a scientist — a first rate magician — organise moderately priced journeys into the Past?
My friends & I would love to spend a week in Paris (under the Consulate, or even, under Louis XI).
I really think this should be seriously looked at!
Do you know this scientist, by any chance?

Spells
When I wish:
...I live in France
"in the days of Charlemagne."
thanks to a friend of mine who is a Wizard...
   (Return to the Past)

Do not let us forget what we owe to Music-Hall & to the Circus. That is where the newest creations, tendencies & curiosities of our craft come from.
Music-Hall & the Circus have the spirit of innovation.

Artists have no right to take up their listener's time pointlessly.
Artists are certainly to be respected, but listeners even more so.
The public worships Ennui. For them, Ennui is mysterious & profound.
A curious thing: the listener is defenceless against boredom. Boredom tames him.
Why is it easier to bore people than to amuse them?

He dances like an angel, just as well backwards as forwards.

Let us be artists without trying.
Ideas can get by without Art.
We should be wary of Art: it is often merely Virtuosity.

Matter (Idea) & Manpower (Writing)
Manpower is often of better quality than Matter.
To have a feeling for harmony means to have a feeling for tone.
Serious examination of a melody will always, for the student, be an excellent *harmonic* exercise.
A melody does not have *its own harmony*, any more than a countryside has *its own colour*. The harmonic situation of a melody is infinite because a melody is expression within the expression.
Do not forget that the melody is the Idea, the contour, as much as it is the form & the subject-matter of a work. Harmony is a form of lighting, setting the object off, reflecting it.

In composition, the parts no longer have "school" relationships between them. School has a gymnastic purpose, that is all; composition has an aesthetic purpose in which taste alone plays a role.
Do not let us confuse things. Knowledge of grammar does not mean knowledge of literature; it can help or be kept at arm's length by the will & responsibility of the writer. Musical grammar is no more & no less than grammar.

An artist's craft can be criticised only if he is continuing a system. Where there is a new form & new writing, there is a new craft.

To talk about this "craft" calls for great prudence & — in any case — a great deal of knowledge.

Who possesses this knowledge? What a mistake!!!

Because, many artists lack general ideas & even specific ideas.

Masters stand out for their ideas, their craft is there as a simple means to an end, that is all. It is their ideas which last.

Which is what makes it seem natural & always right.

Bach's craft is not an exercise in counterpoint. This craft would be mistaken in a school exercise: in composition it is perfect.

Who established the truths which regulate Art? Who?

The Masters? They had no right to & it is improper to attribute to them the power. They all had professional problems to complain about. Take Rodin, Manet, Debussy, etc. Masters are not taken on in the gendarmerie, any more than as school teachers or other magistrates.

If I were rich I'd be afraid of losing my money.

My dear Communist friends (I am a member of the Arcueil *Soviet*) are, when it comes to art, disconcertingly *Bourgeois*... I found it impossible to go on with a column in *L'Humanité*... *Le Gaulois* — I mean it — is more advanced than them.

Sigh:... Good old Debussy was after all a different sort from all these people together.

Quite so, Sir, there will not be any more wars, we have just seen the last one... How bored people will be!

The war cost 10 to 15 million men.

What is a man?

Simply an amalgam of molecules... & pellicles...

All the years I was young people said to me: "You will see when you are 50." I am 50. I haven't seen anything.[90]

Ravel refuses the Legion d'Honneur, but all his music accepts it.[91]

I absolutely agree with our opponents. It is regrettable to see artists advertising. And yet Beethoven was not at all clumsy about publicity. That is what made him well-known, I believe.

The centre of Paris is France — with her colonies, of course.

Jazz tells the story of its pain — & *"we could not care less..."* That is why it is *beautiful, real...*

   No Barracks
I never attack Debussy. It is just the *debussystes* that bother me. There is no school of Satie. *Satisme* could
   never exist. It would find me against it.
In art, there should never be slavery. I have always made an effort to put followers off the scent, by both
   the form & the essentials of each new work. That is the only way for an artist to avoid becoming the
   head of a school, and therefore a swot.
Let us thank Cocteau for helping us to climb out of the provincial & professorial habituation to boredom
   of recent impressionist music.[92]

   His wife told me:
   My husband is very clean... Just think, he used to clean out trenches.

      At the moment I do not have much appetite... I eat with the tips of my teeth... Before long I
      will — perhaps — be eating with the tip of my nose.

      The Opera & the Louvre have aspects of both the refrigerator & the ossuary.

There are some artists who want to be buried alive.

   We have plenty of time for being in a cemetery.

   Don't let us be confused
Composers can be divided into swots, & poets. The former impress the public, & critics. As examples
   of poets I would point to Liszt, Chopin, Schubert, Mussorgsky; as a swot, Rimsky-Korsakov.
   Debussy was the classic poet-musician, among his followers are several sorts of swot musicians.
   (D'Indy, though he teaches others to be, is not one.)
Mozart's craft is light, & Beethoven's heavy, which few people understand; but both are poets. That
   is everything.
P.S. Wagner was a dramatic poet.[93]

      Experience is one form of paralysis.

      Some people, young people, are very old for their age.

Youth is quite pretty, as long as it is not old. (One can have a young mind in an old body.)

   Children have natural wisdom: they know everything.

Remember that children are younger than a lot of old men.

An aesthete is a gentleman who prefers spring greens to preserves.

Sign of the times: the Artists have become professionals; the amateurs have become artists.

Spiders like Music as do most of our composers.

I'd like to play with a grandly-hung piano.[94]

It is not nice to talk about the crotch of the question.[95]

People who do not love Wagner do not love France... Didn't you know Wagner was French? — from Leipsick... But he was...
Have you forgotten?... Already?... You?... a patriot?...[96]

Whether I am French?
Of course... What makes you think a man of my age might not be French?...
You surprise me....[97]

No: Saint-Saëns is not German... He is just a little "hard" in the head... & gets things back to front, that is all... But he's a sound chap, I'll have you know... At his age, one can say what one likes... What difference can it make?[98]

He is really a man of character — the Printing sort, I mean.

The more I know about men, the more I admire dogs.

He who loves me, loves my dog.

Advice (for family meetings). Lying flat on your stomach is absolutely fine...
However, this position is inconvenient for licking the hand of the person who is kicking your backside.[99]

Advice: Do not breathe without boiling your air beforehand.
...If you want to live long, live old....
.....No more short hair: tear it out...[100]

We know how the French love to criticise themselves. ... It is an obsession...

It is such a mania, they continually run themselves down..... & they only admire other people, people who do not come up to their ankle-height, let alone shoulder-height... They are wrong... ...Certainly ... completely wrong...

Are they not therefore the greatest of all peoples? — & are they not the most modest?

Why, yes....

A *Machiavellian* idea: a farm worker has been arrested who tried to derail a train so he could witness a disaster.

Machiavelli had some funny ideas!... What a creep!...

Hidden corners of my life

Often, I regret having come into this base world, myself; not that I hate the world. No... I like the world, the social world & even the twilit world, being myself a sort of twilight demi-mondain.

But what did I come to do upon this earthy, earthly, Earth?

Do I have duties to perform here? Did I come to carry out a mission — a commission?

Was I sent to enjoy myself? to have a little change of scene?... to forget the hardships of a world beyond, of which I remember nothing? Am I not an intruder here?

How can I answer all these questions?

Thinking it was the right thing to do, almost as soon as I arrived down here, I started playing snatches of Music which I made up myself...

All my troubles stem from this....

"Yes, Sir, I fought in the hundred years' war," the venerable old gentleman was telling me. I have to admit it did not interest me.

Man claims he was made in the image of God.
After all, it could be true.

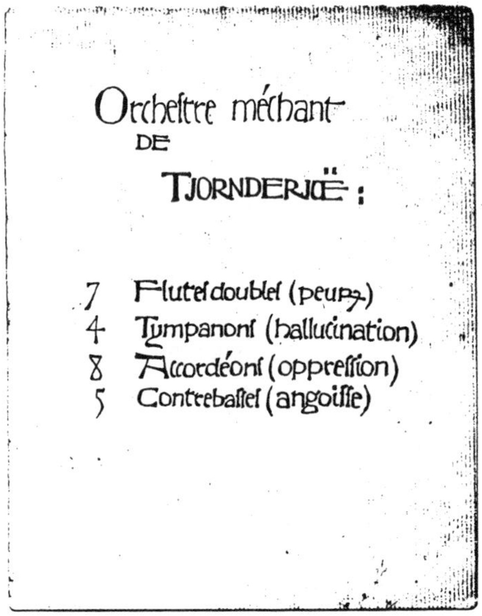

Orcheſtre méchant
DE
TJORNDERJOË :

7 Flutes doubles (peurʒ)
4 Tympanons (hallucination)
8 Accordéons (oppreſſion)
5 Contrebaſſes (angoiſſe)

Plutonia / vast new country in Central Africa / 500, 000, 000, 000 inhabitants! / Sorcerer's Trick / The blackest Negroes in the World

Republic of Spitzberg / States of the Devil / La Baie. St. Léon. Portville. Dune. Richebourg

North Indies Archipelago / Redskins called: Flat Heads, Chatterbox, Uncouth, Thick-Neck & Macacos, Wet Beaks, Terracotta, Parrot & Baboon, Swaggerswill, Tiger's Eyes, Grasshoppers & Waiters' Aprons

New Africa (Neo-Africans) / Sixth Part of the World. Sorcerer's Trick. / 5,000,000,000 inhabitants. / The blackest Negroes in the World, very Savage. / Fabulous Land. Unknown Seas

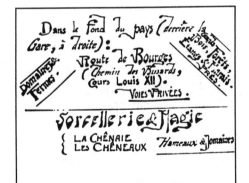

In the heart of the Country (on the right, behind the Station). / Road for Bourges (Buzzards Way, Louis XII Drive). Private Driveway. / Estates and Farms. Deep Woods, Forests, Ponds and Marsh, Meadows / Sorcery and Magic. The Oaks. The Soaks. Hamlets and Estates

⚑ Nasty Orchestra from Tjornderjöe:
7 Double flutes (fear)
4 Trombones (sighs & groans)
8 Accordeons (oppressions)
5 Basset Horns (forlorn)

155

VALLÉE DU VOIR:
Château, parc, terrasses & Ferme de la Baronnie de BIVRY (Henri IV). Etangs, rivières & bois. Moulin à eau. Hameau & vieille église. du XIe. Lavoir public. Louvois y habita (1667).

Look Valley / Castle, Park, Terraces and Farms of the Barony of Bivry (Henri IV). / Ponds, Rivers and Woods. / Watermill. / Hamlet and Old Church XIth Century. / Public Washhouse. / Louvois lived here (1667)

Ouchessin Valley, belonging to a Sorcerer / Castle (Henri IV). Grounds, Terraces and Farms of Ouches. Forest, Ponds, Rivers and Woods. Watermill, Manor (1516). Abbey (1234). Hamlet. Old Church (XIIIth Century) and Pretty Vicarage. Public Washhouse. Lovely Farmland and Vast Marshes

À un Sorcier
VALLÉE DE L'OUCHESSIN
Château (Henri IV); parc, terrasses & Fermes d'OUCHES. FORÊT, étangs, rivières & bois. Moulin à eau. Manoir (1516), Abbaye (1234). Hameau; vieille église (XIIIe) & joli presbytère. Lavoir public. Belles prairies & vastes marais.

Grandeur de Tous
Anarchie despotique
République puis
EMPIRE du TRAVAIL
France, Iles Britanniques, Belgique & Hollande, Germanie, Helvétie, le Nord de l'Italie, péninsule Hispanique, le Canada, l'Afrique septentrionale, la Syrie & l'Asie-Mineure, Chypre, Malte, l'Arabie & la Perse.
ASSERVISSEMENT LIBÉRAL
Résignation volontaire du Peuple
République du Peuple / Empire du Peuple

Greatness for All / Despotic Anarchy / Republic then Empire of Work. / Republic of the People. / Empire of the People. / France, British Isles, Germania, Helvetia, Northern Italy, Iberian Peninsular, Canada, North Africa, Syria and Asia Minor, Cyprus, Malta, Arabia and Persia. / Liberal Subjection. / Voluntary Resignation of the People

Le Sorcier acquereur mystérieux des Territoires de Bagneux, d'Arcueil-Cachan, de Gentilly-Bicêtre, de Villejuif, & de Chevilly.
Un Despote Invisible & Secret
1839-78
* Et influence sur ceux de Montrouge & Darnétal.
Plus les 2/5 du territoire de Rouen & tout celui de Fécamp et leurs banlieues & voisinage.

Valley of Cheek / Land of "Hugeness." Everything: Enormous. / Castle, Grounds, Terraces and Farm "The Plain" (1596). / Ponds, Rivers and Woods. Marsh. / Belonging to the Devil

Invisible Secret Despot (1839-78) / The mysterious Sorcerer, Purchaser of the territories of Bagneux, Arcueil-Cachan, Gentilly-Bicêtre, Villejuif and Chevilly / (with influence over those of Montrouge and Darnetal) / plus two fifths of the territory of Rouen and all that of Fécamp and their suburbs and surroundings

VALLÉE DU TOUPET
Contrée du "gigantesque"
Tout: ÉNORME
Château, parc, terrasses & Ferme de PLAT (1596)
Etangs, rivières & bois. Marais.
Propriété du Diable.

156

A Conqueror... / from time to time... Bastard-Heart devastates a corner of the World,... and disappears... Is he... the Devil?

Un Conquérant: ....
.... De temps en temps,.. CŒUR-DE-VACHE "désole" un "coin" du Monde ,.... & disparaît .....Est-ce le ..... DIABLE ?...

BRUTES DE GUERRE, hordes de faux patriotes, pillards, assassins & traîtres. Bandes terribles.

Brutes of War. Hordes of Fake Patriots. Pillagers, Murderers and Traitors. Terrible Gangs

racloirs frappeurs enfonceurs } Engins de guerre du Dr Lapin (ustensiles dévastateurs & comiques)

Scrapers Pummellers Holers / Dr Rabbit's War Machines (Devastating & Comic Utensils)

DÉPECEURS, terribles hordes de pillards modernes surgissant à l'improviste & disparaissant de même. Horrible & cruelle soldatesque.

Meat-Cutters, terrible Hordes of Modern Pillagers, popping up out of nowhere and disappearing as quickly. Horrible and cruel Soldiery

COUVERCLES ABSORBEURS CONSUMANTS terribles engins de guerre du sergent PUÇON l'inhumain (Cuit & désosse plus de 10,000 hommes à la seconde.)

Consuming Absorbent Lids / Sergeant Puçon the inhuman's terrible War Machines (cook and bone more than 10,000 men per second)

Bandes Féroces de FAUX SOLDATS pillant & tuant sans pitié.

Savage Bands of Fake Soldiers pillaging and killing pitilessly

TRANSFORMATEURS ABSORBEURS INVISIBLES Engin de guerre du professeur QUINT

Société des BOULES de l'ingénieur La Bique, en fer incandescent; énormes masses de feu courant en tous sens, écrasant tout sur leur passage. Canons-formateurs

Mr Nag (Engineer)'s Red-hot Iron Ball Company. Great Masses of Fire running in every direction, crushing everything in their path. / Training-Cannons

Invisible Transformer Absorbers / Professor Quint's War Machine

Sorcerer Doctor Fakelong's Military
Rats & Crows

**RATS &
CORBEAUX
militaires
du Docteur
FAUXLONG
Sorcier**

Picot the Magician's Lead Soldiers /
Can make themselves invisible; climb up
the walls; walk on the water; jump over
houses

**LES SOLDATS
DE PLOMB
du magicien
PICOT
savent se rendre
invisibles ; grimper le
long des murs ; sauter
par dessus les
maisons.**

The Old King's Department Store

**GRANDS MAGASINS
DU
VIEUX ROI**

Dr X***'s Army & Navy / Ridiculous
thing / (Comic Sorcery)./ Terror
through Farce

**ARMÉES DE
TERRE & DE MER
du Dr X •••
Ridicule chose
(Sorcellerie
comique)
LA TERREUR PAR
LE COCASSE**

Saddle (& Draught) Oxen / Speed. /
Lightness / Strength

**BŒUFS
DE SELLE (& TRAIT)
Rapidité
Légèreté
Force**

(Doctor Field-Mouse) / Mechanised
Armies / of Carabus the Enchanter, in
the service of Prince Joseph-Napoleon
Bonaparte, descendent of the phony
King of Rome

**(Docteur Mulot)
ARMÉES MÉCANIQUES
de l'Enchanteur CARABUS
au service du Prince
JOSEPH ~ NAPOLÉON
BONAPARTE
descendant du faux roi de
Rome.**

Grand Mobile Theatre / Entirely built
in Stone and Cast Iron. Superb
Monument. / Iron Stage Sets. / Buffet /
Orchestra. / Amateur Clubs

Globus / Immense Town-house, entirely in cast iron, Gothic style./ Height of Luxury. / Unprecedented!

Salle Madsen / Pianos by Madsen (of Copenhagen) / Agent: A Böttern

The Proud Little Girl's Big Store

The Wonderful White Pine[102] Inn / A sort of Priory-Farm (Gift of the Devil)

Engineer-Forger / All fields. / Better than the real thing

The Wild Bird Inn / Belonging to Magician. / XIIth Century style. In cast iron. / Delightful fairy-tale Courtyard

Sorcerer / Grain and Fodder Broker / Quai Valmy (XIth arr.)

The Red Skin[103] Inn

Rich Turkish House in Cast Iron. /
(Gift from the Devil)

Medieval private Hamlet, fanciful,
enclosed within high walls

The Great Black Sun Inn / Boulevard
Jourdan / Belonging to a wizard

Splendid Gothic Manor in Cast Iron
Grounds and Outbuildings

Retirement Home for Negroes /
Director. General Overseer. Bursar.
Overseers (4). / Chief Attendant.
Deputy Chief Attendant. Attendants
(10) / Inmates (20) / Fondation Juponot
/ Governing Body: Chairman;Vice-
Chairman. Board Members (6)

Ugly Old House Built of Lead (XIIth
Century). Used as Grocery Shop, with
Small Yard and Back-Garden. /
Belonging to a Magician: / Olecoq
(Henri)

160

CONFORTABLE & VIEILLE MAISON borgne, en fonte, d'aspect terrifiant, avec un méchant jardin. VIEUX MEUBLES GROSSIERS (— A un Sorcier)

Comfortable Old House of ill repute in Cast Iron. / Terrifying Appearance, / Beware of the Garden. / Crude Old Furniture. / (Belonging to a Wizard)

Gros Château gothique en fonte, avec Parc lourd & disgracieux. DÉPENDANCES

Big Gothic Castle / in cast iron, with heavy, graceless Park. / Outbuildings

Beau Prieuré roman, en fonte, avec parc & DÉPENDANCES.

Lovely Romanesque Priory in Cast Iron, with Grounds and Outbuildings

PETIT PARC; Terrible & Brutal Château, genre gothique, en fonte; & DÉPENDANCES.

Small Park; / Terrible, Brutal / Castle, / gothic style, / in cast iron; & / Outbuildings

seigneurial Chalet suisse, tout en grès RICHE JARDIN (Don du Diable) & 3 Villas normandes d'un goût exquis

Manorial Swiss Chalet, entirely built in Sandstone. Well-stocked Garden (Gift from the Devil) and three Norman Villas in exquisite taste

Enormous, Beautiful Castle / Medieval Style / cast iron

Prétentieux Château genre gothique, en fonte; avec PETIT PARC insolent; & nobles Dépendances. (Marquis de Valois) Sorcier

ÉNORME & BEAU Château genre médiéval en fonte

Pretentious Castle / gothic style, in cast iron; with Small insolent Park; & lordly Out-buildings. / (Marquis de Valois) / Sorcerer

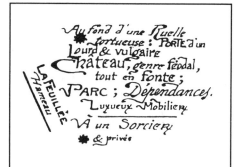

Villa Paul / (Former prison) / Shapeless, grandiose, feudal, abandoned Castle (XIIth C) (1113), hacked out of sandstone block. Parts made of crude cast iron: Haunted. Built by the Devil's son deep in distant woods. Enclosed with walls. Private driveways. / Rivers, Ponds, Meadows

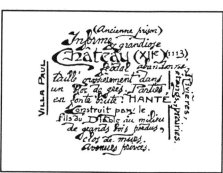

At the bottom of a tortuous Alley: Gate of a Heavy, common Castle, feudal style, all in cast iron; / The Bower / Hamlet / Park; Outbuildings. Sumptuous Furnishings / Belonging to a Sorcerer / private

Strange, grandiose, feudal Castle XIIth C, abandoned, built in 1113, in one night, by the Devil's son for his pretty mistress. Deep in great ancient distant woods; rivers, ponds, lovely meadows. All enclosed with great long walls; outer Avenues all private: Villa Paul. Luxuriously restored

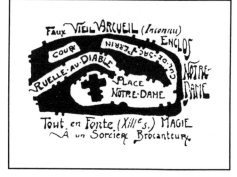

Piece of Parkland, & Enormous, Vulgar, modern Castle, very XIIIth Century. / entirely in cast iron / Austere furnishings: idem. / ARCUEIL: Roman Avenue / (Abandoned) / Fake Ruins belonging to a Sorcerer

False Old Arcueil (Unknown) / All made of Cast Iron (XIIIth Century). Magic. Belonging to a Junk-Dealer Sorcerer. / Notre Dame Close: Courtyard. Perrin Alley, Cul-de-sac. Devil's Alley. Notre Dame Square.

Belonging to a sorcerer. / Sweet-Water-Under-Wood. / Tucked away: on the main road / Forest, Castle & Farm / (XVth Century) in cast iron / Period furnishings

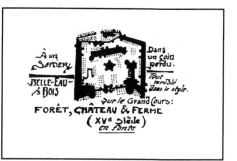

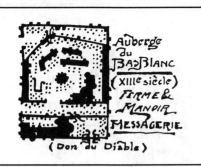

The White Stocking Inn / Farm and Manor House (XIIIth Century) / Coaching Post / (Gift of the Devil)

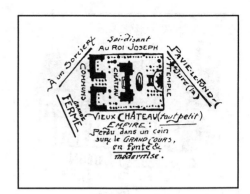

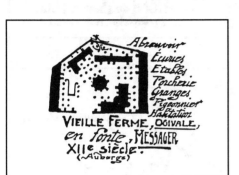

Drinking-trough / Stables / Cow-sheds / Pigsty / Barns / Dovecote / Dwelling / Old Farm, Early Gothic, in cast iron, Messenger XIIth century. / (Inn)

Belongs to a Sorcerer / Big Farm / Pavia-the -Bottom (Jure) / Forge-On-The-Bubble / The White Pine Inn / Manor & Farm (1253) / Entirely in cast iron / Gift of the Devil to his Godson

Small House in cast iron, very XIIIth Century (1 storey) Attics. Fine Cellars / Library. Bedr. Yard. Pantry. Kitchen. Vault

Said to have been King Joseph's Old (tiny) Castle / Empire Style: Hidden away on the Main Road, built in cast iron & modernised / Temple. Castle. Commons

Castle & Old Farm XIIth century in cast iron / (Sensational)

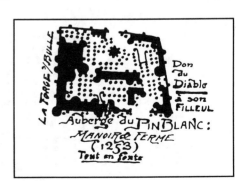

Baron Pulard's Town House / Built
entirely in cast iron

Curious House / entirely in cast iron
(XVIth C) / Belongs to a Sorcerer

In an alley: / Old House / Unique ? in
cast iron / XIIth & XVth centuries /
(modernised) / belongs to a sorcerer /
Yard & Gardens

Entirely in cast iron XXIIIth C

Cellars;	Cellars;
Hall; &	Kitchen; &
Bedroom;	Study;
& Attic;	& Attic &
Cell	Cell

Fake Castle / Wooded grounds / Low-
Towers Alley / Magic

164

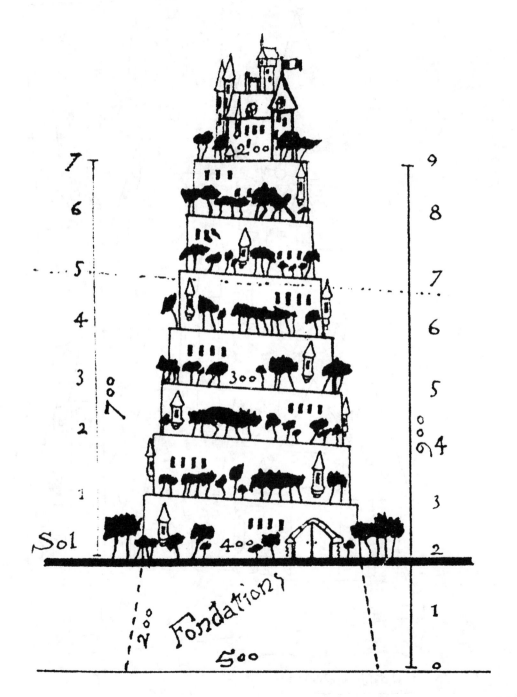

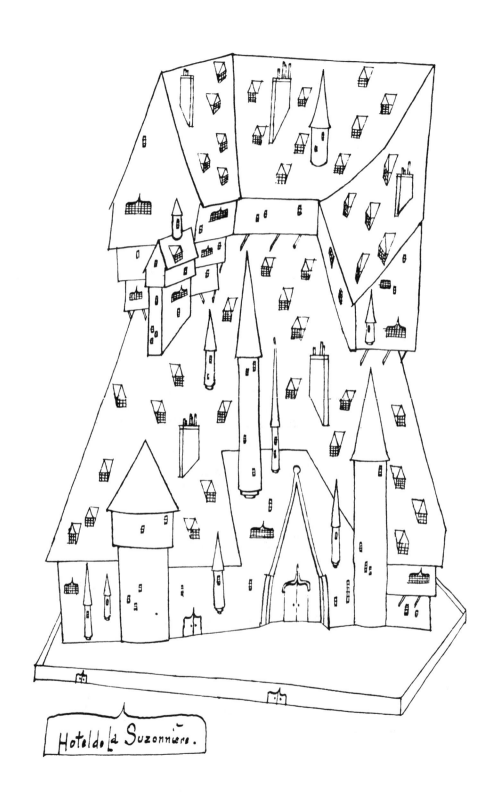

Hotel de La Suzonnière.

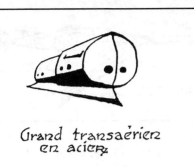

Grand transaérien
en acier.

"The Star" / Large Five-Master / Polar Excursions

GRAND CINQ-MATS
"L'ÉTOILE"
EXCURSIONS POLAIRES

Large transaerial liner / made of steel

"The Invisible" / Large transaerial liner / by Dr Paillon — Sorcerer

"L'invisible"
Grand transaérien
du Dr PAILLON — Sorcier

"The Flighty" / large Five-Master / (Polar Excursions)

(EXCURSIONS POLAIRES)
GRAND CINQ-MATS
"VOLAGE"

Modern Transaerial Liner / Republic Of Spitzberg / Boreans / (1876) St George capital / Frigorenhavn / Its Magic Armies / Its Magic Fleets / Its Magic Trade & Its Magic Industry

MODERNE
TRANSAÉRIEN
RÉPUBLIQUE DU SPITZBERG
BORÉENS
(1876) St Georges Capitale
Frigorenhavn
SES ARMÉES MAGIQUES
SES FLOTTES
SON COMMERCE &
SON INDUSTRIE

Large Five-Master

GRAND
CINQ-MATS

Big transaerial liners by W.B. Sound, sorcerer. (Spitzberg) / States Of Spitzberg / (St George Capital) / (Boreans) / Boreal Republic / Cap: Frigorenhavn

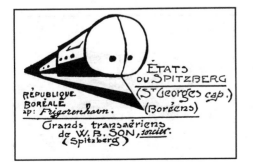

ÉTATS
DU SPITZBERG
(St Georges cap.)
(Boréens)
RÉPUBLIQUE
BORÉALE
ap: Frigorenhavn.
Grands transaériens
de W. B. SON, sorcier.
(Spitzberg)

"St John" / Large Glider made of steel

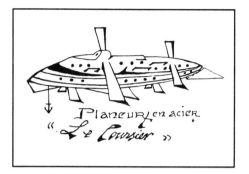

"The Charger"
Glider made of steel.

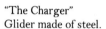

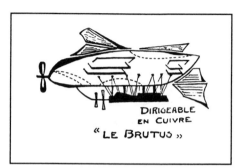

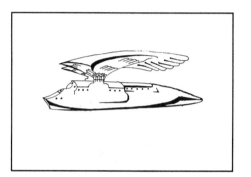

"The Brutus" / Airship Made Of Copper

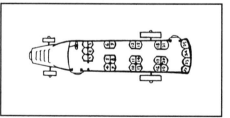

"The Rapid" / Airship made of copper

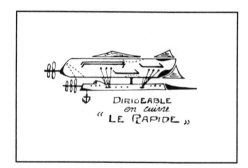

"The Salmon" / Airship made of copper

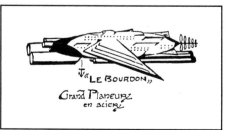

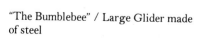

"The Bumblebee" / Large Glider made of steel

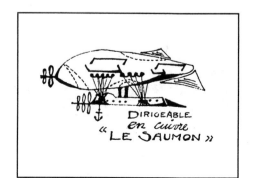

Dates in inverted commas appear on the original mss

1. Note in the margin of the original edition of *Heures séculaires & instantanées*, for piano, E. Demets, Paris, 1917. Later editions by Max Eschig, like all Satie's works first published by Demets. This note of Satie's can be equally applied to all the texts in this section.

Contamine de Latour relates (in *Erik Satie intime, Souvenirs de jeunesse, Comœdia* 3/5/6 Aug 1925; see *Satie Remembered*, p. 27), how Satie decided one day, with great jubilation, to replace the standard tempo marks (*lent, grave,* etc.) with his own made-up expressions (*Without pride, With amazement, Even whiter if possible,* etc.) which addressed the pianist's feelings rather than his or her technique.

After meeting the great pianist Ricardo Viñes, late in 1912, and making him a privileged accomplice for a number of years, Satie — now in the middle of this "fantasist" period" — started to enjoy thinking up performance indications and tempo marks which mixed poetic humour with a taste for the absurd (*On yellowing velvet, On the tips of your back teeth, Light as an egg*), and which seem to be driven by a desire to disrupt the player's presumably rational approach, in order to make him more easily receptive. These performance indications ended up developing to the point where they began to look like little stories, and charmed a number of pianists and concert organisers to the extent that they started reading them out in the course of musical performance. This provoked the wrath of Satie who could not tolerate these voices over the delivery of his music, whether or not the words were his own work. He declared once and for all that "These indications are a secret between the performer and myself."

2. From the first edition of *Descriptions automatiques*, "April 1913," for piano, E. Demets, Paris, 1913.

This is the first of a series of pieces constructed using "quotations" from familiar refrains: arias from operetta, children's songs, popular tunes, etc. The tempo marks which seem on the surface to be arranged so as to evoke a particular atmosphere, are in fact hidden clues to the musical quotations contained in the corresponding passages. *On a Vessel* refers to the children's song *Maman, les p'tits bateaux ont-ils des jambes?* (Mummy, do little boats have legs?); *On a Lantern* alludes to the refrain of *Dansons la Carmagnole,* a song from the Revolution which includes the words *"Les Aristocrates à la Lanterne"* (String up the aristos on the lamp-post); and the score of *On a Helmet* quotes not only the military fanfare *En Avant,* but also a piece by Debussy inspired by an eccentric clown who went by the name of *General Lavine.*

3. From the first edition of *Embryons desséchés,* "June-July 1913," for piano. E. Demets, Paris, 1913.

The reason for observing Holothuria in "St-Malo bay" is that the music quotes a romance that was famous at the time: *Mon Rocher de Saint Malo* by Gustave Lemoine and Loïsa Puget. The reason the Edriophthalma weep, is because the music is playing Chopin's *Marche funèbre.* While the "advisor" of the Podophthalma appears along with the tune of *Ah! ne courez donc pas comme ça* (Oh! Do not run around like that) from the operetta *La Mascotte* by Edmond Audran.

4. From the first edition of *Chapitres tournés en tous sens,* "August-September 1913" E. Demets, Paris, 1913.

She Who Talks Too Much relates to a quotation from the tune of *Ne parle pas, Rose, je t'en supplie* (Rose, do not speak, I beg you) from the operetta *Les Dragons de Villars,* by Aimé Maillart. *The Man Who Carries Big Stones,* straining to bear the featherlight weight of a pumice stone, is accompanied by *Vive la Paresse* (Long Live Laziness) from the operetta *Rip* by Robert Planquette.

Meanwhile the "Prisoners" several centuries apart (the prophet Jonah in the belly of the whale, and the adventurer Jean-Henry de Latude in the gaols of Louis XV, because of his plotting against Madame de Pompadour), "lament" to the tune of *Nous n'irons plus aux bois* (We shan't go down to the woods no more), a popular song which Debussy had already quoted in *Jardins sous la pluie* (as Satie implicitly recognises by dedicating this piece to his friend's wife).

5. From the first edition of *Vieux Sequins & Vieilles Cuirasses,* "September 1913", E. Demets, Paris, 1913.

At the Gold Merchant's is a crazy version of the tune to *La Ronde du Veau d'Or* (The Dance of the Golden Calf) from Gounod's *Faust.* A military march called *Aux champs* (To the field of battle), is the inspiration for the *Dance in Armour.* Two children's refrains *Marlbrouk s'en va-t-en guerre* (Marlborough is off to war) and *Le Bon roi Dagobert* (Good King Dagobert) are overlaid to produce the tiny child's "nightmare," after its grandfather has told the story (rather confusedly) of the *Defeat of the Cimbrians.*

6. From the manuscript in the Bibliothèque Nationale de France, Département de la Musique (henceforth referred to as BNF-MUS), MS 9612, sketches (September 1913), which was published posthumously under the title *Trois nouvelles Enfantines,* I. *Le vilain petit Vaurien.* II. *Berceuse.* III. *La gentille Toute petite fille,* Max Eschig, Paris, 1972.

7. From the manuscript dated "27th-28th September 1913," for piano. Private Collection. Hitherto unpublished.

8. From the first edition of *Enfantines, I.,* "20th October 1913" E. Demets, Paris, 1914 (1916).

All these pieces for children, which were written with the smallness of the young players' hands in mind, are embellished with texts suitable for children, in which particular words, colours, or situations are repeated to draw attention to the return of the same musical idea.

9. From the first edition of *Enfantines, II., ibid.,* 1914 (1916).

10. From the first edition of *Enfantines, III., ibid.,* 1914 (1916).

11. From the manuscript BNF-MUS, MS 9627 (10), sketches (May 1914). Hitherto unpublished.

12. From the manuscript: BNF-MUS, MS 9615 (3), sketches.

13. *Ibid.,* MS 9625 (1) sketches:

14. From the first edition of *Sports & Divertissements,* "14th March to 20th May 1914," Publications Lucien Vogel, Paris (1923).

Here again the text corresponds to musical quotations. *The Bride's Reveille* mixes up the army wake-up call with the refrain from *Frère Jacques, dormez-vous?* The "losers" at *The Races* withdraw in shame to the tune of the Marseillaise, which says a lot about Satie's military-patriotic sentiments; while the song *Au clair de la lune, mon ami Pierrot* accompanies the frustrated sighing of the lover who "would like to be on the moon," but is not having much success in his *Flirting.*

All these tunes and songs could still be described as "on everyone's lips" in Paris at the beginning of the century, since pecple at the time would go around humming tunes, both at home and in the street; thus the quotations and references actually meant something. For studies of the relation between Satie's music and popular songs, see *A propos d'Erik Satie, Notules incohérentes,* by Léon Guichard, in *Recherches et travaux,* 7, Université de Grenoble, March 1973, and *Erik Satie et la tradition populaire,* Fondation Erik Satie, Musée national des arts et traditions populaires, Paris, 1988.

15. From the first edition of *Heures séculaires & instantanées,* "June-July 1914", Paris, E. Demets, 1917.

"Sir William Grant-Plumot" has never been properly identified. Some see him as the critic Willy, who had for a long time been Satie's great enemy, but they had recently been reconciled. Willy used a number of ghost writers to produce large quantities of lightweight novels published under his name, and a prodigious number of witty, informative articles. He had been publishing without let-up for

several decades. *Plumeau* is a cockade, thus the implication is that "Big Pen" (*Grande Plume*) is flaunting a cockade as a pen.

Shakespeare is another candidate for "Sir William" even if he was never a knight, though Satie might have considered the title a way of paying homage to his immortal renown (which might qualify as "continuous immobility"): a year later Satie composed his *Cinq Grimaces pour "le Songe d'une Nuit d'Eté"* (April 1915). The "good-natured" Louis XI was famously responsible for massacring the Cathars.

16. From the first edition of *Les trois Valses distinguées du Précieux Dégouté,* "July 1914," Rouart Lerolle, Paris, 1916. Later editions by Salabert, like all Satie's works first published by Rouart Lerolle.

The *squeamish pansy* targeted in this triptych was Maurice Ravel, who Satie described elsewhere as "a little doddering dandy." Ravel said of himself that he was "naturally artificial". Besides this aspect of his personality, Satie failed to appreciate the fact that Ravel presented Satie as his precursor. Nor did he appreciate this young man, whom he had known as a teenager, claiming that his *Entretiens de la Belle et la Bête (Ma mère l'Oye)* was the "fourth *Gymnopédie.*" To make quite clear that Ravel had understood nothing about him, Satie "quotes" his first *Gymnopédie* at the faster tempo Ravel so liked, in the second panel of this triptych, *His Pince-Nez,* which comes with an epigraph from Cicero enjoining pubescent youths not to show themselves naked (*Gymnopédie* meaning, in ancient Greek, "naked boy").

17. From the first edition of *Avant-dernières Pensées,* "August to October 1915". Rouart Lerolle, Paris, 1916.

18. From the first edition of *Sonatine bureaucratique;* S. Chapelier, Paris, (July) 1917, later edition by Combre. The third movment's heading is not a mistake, but a combination with *vache,* French for a cow.

19. From the manuscript: BNF-MUS, MS 9609 (2), sketches for the first *Nocturne* (Rouart Lerolle, 1919).The text was not printed in the published edition.

20. BNF-MUS, MS 9576, sketches for a trilogy for piano, inspired by popular novels: *Paul & Virginie, Robinson Crusoé* and *Don Quichotte* (September 1920). For the third panel, Satie planned to use Lamartine's poem *L'Isolement,* which he used not long afterwards for his *Elegy "to the memory of Debussy"* (December 1920).

21. The indications scattered by Satie throughout his piano works, as published; listed here in alphabetical order (apart from those that appear elsewhere in this compilation).

22. Though Satie only signed the music to *Uspud* and credited the

text to his friend, the Catalan poet J.P.Contamine de Latour, in his memoirs the latter made clear that the text was the fruit of a collaboration between them. It was inspired by Flaubert's *Tentation de Saint Antoine*, and Henri Rivière's shadow play of the same name at the *Chat Noir*, but unlike these antecedents this text is free of erotic allusions. Significantly, the highly dramatic action described in the text of *Uspud* is accompanied by music of an Olympian calm — the kind of contrast Satie enjoyed creating, as if he wished to stress the independence of the two expressive forms applied to one subject.

Though they called it a "ballet," the two friends most probably composed *Uspud* for the shadow theatre at the Auberge du Clou, the Cabaret where Satie was employed as "second pianist" at the time; this would explain the many fantasmagorical beings that appear in all three acts, though the hero is presented from the beginning as the "sole character." It would also explain why the piano score contains at various places indications for bringing in "flutes" and "harps" with no further instruction. The music for these shadow plays, anticipating the music for silent films, was usually played on a harmonium which could produce the sounds of various instruments, and was sometimes also accompanied with free improvisation by musicians in the wings.

However, as a stunt to impress his Montmartre friends, Satie had also succeeded in presenting his ballet to the director of the Paris Opera, having obtained a meeting by threatening him with a duel, no less (see O. Volta, 1989, p. 39-42). Though the meeting was fruitless, it meant he could subsequently declare that *Uspud* had been "presented" at the Opera, even if not "performed."

The night before that meeting the composer worked hard to give "human form" to his manuscript, the first version being mixed up with correspondence between the authors (see O. Volta, 1989, p. 36-37) and testimonials to the value of the work issuing from historical figures who expressed themselves "by means of a spirit table". This second, shorter, cleaned up version, now in the Bibliothèque Nationale de France (MUS-MS 9631), was published by Salabert in 1970.

Being a dedicated perfectionist, Satie further re-worked the piece with one or two variations before publishing it in 1893 with the help of a whip-round by his friends. We publish here translations of both the first and the third version of the text, one after the other. The text of the first version is taken from the manuscript (with text and music integrated) written out by hand by Erik Satie (except for the correspondence mentioned earlier), on fifty two pages numbered by him in a music exercise book with a dark green cover, bought at the "stationers and binders

H. Lard, Maison Lard-Esnault, founded in 1795, 25 Rue Feydeau, in Paris". (Private collection.)

The text of the third version is from the brochure printed at Satie's behest by the Imprimerie artistique, E. Woestendieck directeur, 42 Rue de la Tour d'Auvergne (Archives de la Fondation Erik Satie).

This 16 page brochure on Oxford laid paper, 22 x 14 cm, is entirely printed in lower case, except for the title and dedication — probably a first in the history of printing. The brochure is illustrated with four "fragments" of the score, and bears on the cover a medallion with the profile of the two authors drawn by Suzanne Valadon, who was having an affair with the composer at the time.

Two years later Satie produced a further *Uspud* in the form of a portfolio (eight pages, 9 x 11 cm, undated) this time with only the musical fragments, with the same medallion on the cover, but without the signature, Satie having separated from Valadon in the meantime.

23. From the manuscript, BNF-MUS: MS 9593 (3).

Two other works from this period — *Three Love Poems*, and *Thoughts-Before-Last* — feature the theme of an old man in love with a young woman, which is the subject of this ballet libretto; not even sketches for the music have been found.

24. From the manuscript, BNF-MUS, Jane Bathori collection.

Satie had initially planned to call No. 2 "No. 3" and vice versa (see Catalogue entry for 20 November-2 December, 1914, below) but gave up this joke both in the final ms. and in the published version (Rouart Lerolle, 1916, then Salabert).

It is worth noting that the verses which are apparently humorous and in which the meaning is often merely the result of the rhyme, are to be sung in the manner of the Gregorian chant *Victimae paschali laudes* which Satie actually uses in the score (cf. Léon Guichard, *Erik Satie et la musique grégorienne*, in *La Revue Musicale*, 169, 15 November 1936).

He says in his cryptic introduction to the work that it is "the love of Love" — which is to say, love of God — that medieval troubadours were really singing about, on the pretext of serenades to the women they loved. So love of Love is at the heart of these poems dedicated by an elderly lover (Satie himself, perhaps?) to his "pretty tripping crotchet."

25. From the manuscript of the score for voice and piano, written out on twenty six sheets of music paper measuring 36 x 28 cm, numbered 8 to 53. In the collection of the Comte et Comtesse Jean de Polignac, Monaco. The same text appears on the orchestral score (same collection).

The text of Satie's *Socrate* might be considered the first example of a new literary genre, consisting of a collage of extracts from the already existing works of another author, arranged in their original succession without a single new word being added. Satie took three of Plato's dialogues: *The Symposium*, *The Phaedrus*, and *The Phaedo*, and selected four extracts from chapter 32 of the *Symposium* (altogether 39 chapters), plus two extracts from chapters 33 and 38. He picked out two extracts from chapter 4 of the *Phaedrus* (64 chapters), and one from chapter 5; and from the *Phaedo* (67 chapters), four extracts from chapter 33, two from chapter 35, three from chapter 38, two from chapter 65, and one from chapter 67.

Satie joined these fragments in the order in which they appear, to make three quite new texts which become the three panels of a triptych telling the story of Socrates' life, rather in the form of early altar pieces. The first panel paints his portrait, the second describes his way of life in the form of a walk beside the river with a disciple; and the third, the manner of his dying.

So that the connection with Plato's books should not be forgotten, Satie requests that the text be sung "reading" and he even had the work performed in a bookshop (Adrienne Monnier's *Maison des Amis des Livres*, on 21 March 1919). In order to make it quite clear that a book is being read, and avoid any risk of the characters being identified with the performers, Satie recommended that *Socrates* be sung by one, two or, if possible, four female voices.

26. Translator's note. I have left spaces to indicate the pauses in the vocal score (see p. 13).

27. From the manuscript, on twenty nine sheets written on one side only, in a school exercise book with a mauve cover, labelled *Omnium*, 22 x 17.5 cm, Paris, Galerie Louise Leiris, Kahnweiler Archive. The seven dances are taken from the first edition, (Galerie Simon, Paris, August 1921).

Satie wrote a clean copy of this manuscript especially for the edition published by the Galerie Simon (run by Daniel-Henry Kahnweiler, who handled the cubists' paintings). The first ms. of the work, which was completed in February 1913, had been lost in a taxi before the first private performance of the play, at the house of the composer Roland Manuel's parents, the date of which varies according to the account between late 1913 and early 1914.

Satie himself played on the piano the *Seven little tiny dances* which interleave the acts, and placed pieces of paper between the piano strings to achieve a sound as "stuffed" as the monkey which was supposed to do the dances.

A misprint in the first edition meant that for years Baron Medusa (which means "Baron Jellyfish" in French), said he belonged to the family of the "cephalids," while in fact, when he wants to say (p. 93) that jellyfish belong to the order of the "acalephs," he pretends to get the word wrong and says "acephalous" instead, which is to say the "headless" creatures that Satie was particularly fond of, as they escape the bounds of cartesianism.

28. *Le Coeur*, II, 6-7, September-October 1893, p. 11-12.

After a brief participation in the Sâr Péladan's Rose+Croix, for whose events he composed several works, Satie decided to found his own church, intended to "combat society by means of music and painting" (cf. Santiago Rusiñol, *Impresiones de Arte*, in *Obres completes*, Selecta, Barcelona, 1976, II, 740). He gave himself the title of *"parcier,"* an old word for *"partiaire,"* meaning one who has a share of something — he actually says he is *"parcier de Dieu,"* or one with a share in God — and set up his church in his *placard* or "cupboard" at 6, Rue Cortot.

29. *Le Menestrel*, LX, 23, 10 June 1894, p. 23.

This "open letter" addressed to the Academician and composer Camille Saint-Saëns, was written by Erik Satie on his twenty-eighth birthday, when he was for the second time applying for a chair in the Académie des Beaux Arts (see p. 102).

30. *Cartulaire*, 2, 63, June 1895, p. 2.

The Metropolitan Church of Art of Jesus Leader, founded by Satie in October 1893 (see above, note 28), nearly two years later acquired a press organ, the *Cartulaire*, which lasted for only two issues. Satie was the only contributor to this broadsheet, and used various pseudonyms. The spirit of the articles is generally what he thought would suit a member of the ecclesiastical hierarchy.

31. Caroline Rémy (1817-1929), the spiritual daughter of the Revolutionary journalist Jules Vallès, and wife of Dr Adrien Guebhardt, the backer of the *Cri du Peuple* wrote rebellious articles under the pseudonym of Séverin, and later Séverine, in defence of the poor, the downtrodden and the persecuted, which included Captain Dreyfus.

32. Saint François de Paule (Francesco Martotilla, 1416-1507) was the Calabrian ascetic who founded the Order of Minims, and advocated perpetual Lent. To put his name to a sermon against the poor is a little provocative.

33. From the *Revue musicale S.I.M*, VIII, 4, 15 April 1912, p. 69.

Satie has a note after the words "not a musician," which

refs the reader to a contemporary publication: O. Séré, *Musiciens français d'aujourd'hui*, p.138. These *Mémoires d'un Amnesique* are proposed as "fragments" of an already existing work, which in fact never existed. They live up well to their title, given that they never make the slightest allusion to the private life of their author. They were originally conceived as a column in the *Revue musicale S.I.M.*, but continued under the same heading when revived in the literary review *les feuilles libres*.

34. *Ibid.*, VIII, 7-8, July-August 1912, p.83.

35. We have no way of knowing whether Satie refers here to David Teniers the Elder (1582-1649) or to David Teniers the Younger (1610-1690). Both, father and son, were born in Antwerp, and specialised in popular Flemish scenes.

36. *Revue musicale S.I.M*, VIII, 11, November 1912, p.70.

37. Charpentier (1860-1956) composed the popular opera *Louise*.

38. Ernest Guiraud (1837-1892) had been one of Debussy's teachers at the Conservatoire. With regard to Gounod, and Ambroise Thomas, Satie had the opportunity later on to "complete an opera by the former (see Catalogue entry for August-December 1923 below) and give his opinion on the latter (p. 109)

39. Composers Emile Paladilhe (1844-1926), François-Clément Dubois (1837-1924) and Charles Lenepveu (1840-1910) had each won the Prix de Rome before being elected Academicians.

40. The composer Emile Pessard (1843-1917) who, in spite of many approaches, was never elected to the Academy, was also a Prix de Rome, like most of the candidates in this election, with the exception of Satie.

41. *Revue musicale S.I.M.*, IX, 1, 15 January 1913, p.71.

42. *Ibid.*, IX, 2, 15 February 1913, p.69.

43. *Ibid.*, X, 2, 1 February 1914, p.69.

44. Unpublished text, transcribed by Pierre-Daniel Templier at Conrad Satie's, then lost. (Archives de la Fondation Erik Satie.)

45. The Dufayel department store, which even stocked music "ready to play" to accompany silent films, were at the time a symbol of very basic production within the reach of all and sundry.

46. *les feuilles libres*, VI, 35, Jan.-Feb. 1924, pp. 329-331.

47. Emile Vuillermoz (1878-1960) and Louis Laloy (1874-1944) were two music critics whom Satie counted among his "most faithful enemies."

48. The title of this section, "Articulated Articles," has been borrowed from that of a column (*Propos à propos*), which Satie wrote in *les feuilles libres*, between October 1922 and January 1924. The first text *On Being Dizzy* was found among Erik Satie's papers and transcribed by Pierre-Daniel Templier, his first biographer, around 1930. The original has since been lost.

49. *L'Oeil de Veau*, I, February 1912, p. 3.

For his first contribution to this little magazine run by his young friend the composer Roland Manuel (Alexis Roland Manuel Lévy, 1891-1966), and the writer and journalist Gaston Picard (1892-1965), Satie chose to write about Ambroise Thomas (1811-1896), the composer of *Mignon*, who had been director of the Conservatoire National de Musique et de Déclamation when he himself had been a student there. Thomas had judged him to be a "thoroughly insignificant pupil."

Besides getting his own back in this article where he shows as much interest in his former master as in his umbrella, Satie applied for the succession to his seat in the Académie des Beaux Arts in 1896, and used a theme from *Mignon* in one of his pieces that was "not to be listened to" (*Furniture Music*, 1920).

50. Satie's attachment to his umbrella became legendary. He is said to have been seen buying them "in bouquets," and hundreds are said to have been found in his miserable room in Arcueil when he died.

51. *Guide de l'Etranger à Montmartre* (A Visitor's Guide to Montmartre), by Victor Meusy and Edmond Depas, prefaced by Emile Goudeau, dépositaire J. Strauss, Paris, 1900, p. 31-2.

Though this was written at a time when he was "wasting his valuable time to earn a bit of money" as a *tapeur à gages* (pianist) for the Montmartre *chansonniers*, especially Vincent Hyspa (1865-1938) who wrote the words to a number of his songs, Satie carefully avoids naming names in this text, even though it was supposed to celebrate his current companions.

52. Brucolacs are a species of vampire which appear to have been observed in the Greek islands in the XVIIth century. They were the bodies of the excommunicated, taken over by demons athirst for blood, and shared with certain dead saints the characteristic of not decomposing. In addition, in their tombs their skin "becomes stretched taut like a drum, and when you tap it, it gives out the same sound." (Leo Allatius, *De Graecorum hodie quorundam opinationibus*, 1645.)

53. From a manuscript which bears no date or title (August

1917?) given to Roland Manuel by Satie. (Private collection.)

Satie wrote this text after being found guilty in the court of first instance in a libel case brought against him by the critic Jean Poueigh (1876-1958), who considered he had been publicly insulted by the postcard sent him by Satie after he tore apart *Parade*: "Monsieur, you are nothing but an arse, and an arse without any music."

At a meeting at Roland Manuel's, the poet Max Jacob had preached Christian resignation to him in the face of this nasty turn of events. Satie was unable to contain his anger and stormed out without saying goodbye, until his humour resurfaced and he sent this text to his host to apologise.

54. From an untitled ms., submitted to *les feuilles libres* around 1922, and hitherto unpublished. (Archives de la Fondation Erik Satie.)

Presumably inspired by the chaotic and contradictory news coming out of Russia after the October revolution.

55. From a manuscript on one double page, 20 x 15.5 cm. (Private collection.)

Text written for the *Almanach de Cocagne pour l'An 1922*, La Sirène 1922, p. 69. By all accounts Satie was particularly fond of good food (though he was often obliged by his constant lack of money to go without meals), and uses this occasion to remember the first, sweet years of his friendship with Claude Debussy, before "life and the *debussystes*" came between them (p. 122).

56. *Catalogue de Pierre Trémois*, "Libraire-Editeur," No.1, March 1922, p. 3.

Satie had got to know Pierre Trémois, a rich young man with a passion for rare books, at the home of the dancer Caryathis, who was kept by him. Trémois was helped in his shop by Jean Mollet, to whom Apollinaire had given the title of "baron" and who, years later, was elected Vice-Curator of the Collège de 'Pataphysique and addressed by members of the Collège as "His Magnificence."

57. Adrienne Monnier's Maison des Amis des Livres at 7 Rue de l'Odéon, and her neighbour Sylvia Beach's Shakespeare & Co. were meeting places for all the great writers, as well as young literati, in Paris. Satie was probably introduced to them by his friend Léon-Paul Fargue.

58. The Librairie de l'Art Indépendant, which "hid behind its window, rather than displaying" a strange mixture of Symbolist poems and esoteric works, was run by former communard Edmond Bailly, who among other things was the author of a book called *Le Chant des Voyelles*.

This bookshop's logo, designed by Félicien Rops, with the motto of Baudelaire's publisher, Poulet-Malassis, *Non hic piscis omnium* ("not everyone's fish is here"), appeared on the first slim publications of Paul Claudel and André Gide, as well as on one or two pamphlets privately published by Erik Satie.

59. The composer Ernest Chausson (1855-1899), secretary-general of the influential Société Nationale de Musique, produced the first concert performance of two *Gymnopédies* by Erik Satie, orchestrated by Claude Debussy, in 1897.

60. *Catalogue*, 2, April 1922, p. 3.

61. Translator's note. The "reader" of unsolicited play manuscripts sent in to the theatre.

62. This is a popular expression for a deadly blow to the back of the neck. Satie plays on two meanings of the word *père*, used to denote a familiar, usually elderly, character, or an ecclesiastic, as in English.

63. *Catalogue*, 5, October 1922, p. 3.

From the Chat Noir in Montmartre, to La Rotonde in Montparnasse, Satie was a pillar of cabaret, or café society, throughout his life.

64. The humorist Alphonse Allais (1854-1905), who like Satie came from Honfleur, had also written an ironical text on café regulars in his story, *Le Bottin*.

65. Maurice Donnay (1859-1945) had started out declaiming poems and shadow-theatre plays at the Chat Noir, and went on to be elected to the Académie, as successor to the historian Albert Sorel, Satie's father's childhood friend.

66. I have been unable to trace this "great-uncle" in Satie's genealogy.

67. Satie knew Rabelais very well, and drew from him his *Trois petites pièces montées* (see Catalogue entry for January 1920 below).

The preface to *Gargantua* (which quotes, incidentally, the same passage from the *Symposium* as Satie used in his *Portrait of Socrates*) probably prompted the idea of dedicating some of his works "to a dog." Rabelais advised readers — who found themselves baffled by "curious" titles without trying to understand the works hidden behind them — to follow the example of dogs, which are not put off by the unappetising appearance of a bone, but sniff at it and dig around, and do not cease until they have extracted its "substantifick marrow."

68. François Villon (1431-1463?) has retained a reputation as

both a great poet and a great hoodlum.

69. By quoting all these names, Satie shows considerable knowledge of French literary history. The poets Bonaventure Des Periers (c.1500-c.1544), Clément Marot (1496-1544) and the printer-humanist Etienne Dolet (1509-1546), were all defenders of freedom of thought, to the extent that Dolet was burnt at the stake for heresy, and Marot died in exile. They were close friends, and all close to François Rabelais.

70. Jacques Bénigne Bossuet (1627-1704), prelate and theologian; Jean-Baptiste Massillon (1663-1742) priest and rhetorician.

71. Nicolas Boileau (1636-1711), writer and moralist; Jean Racine (1639-1699), the famous dramatic poet; Antoine Furetière (1620-1688), a writer first elected, then expelled from the Académie. Jean de la Fontaine (1621-1695), the famous writer of fables; Claude Chapelle (1628-1686), a poet.

72. Raoul Ponchon: a very popular Montmartre poet and *chansonnier*.

73. From a typescript on a sheet of copy paper 24 x 18 cm, which Satie handed to his American friend Sybil Harris, perhaps hoping to have it published in one of the American magazines to which she had an entrée.

74. Alphonse Karr (1808-1890) was a journalist and writer who was particularly appreciated by Satie's father, and part of Satie's childhood reading.

75. From the manuscript, on ten sheets of paper written on one side, numbered 1 to 10, in a school exercise book.

This piece was written at the request of Sybil Harris who translated it into English and had it published in *Vanity Fair*, X, 6, Feb 1923, p.38 and 88, under the title: *Igor Strawinsky: a Tribute to the Great Russian Composer by an Eminent French Confrère*. (Strawinsky with a w was the pre-war spelling.)

The text is a model of criticism as Satie understood it, without ever having been able to attract it himself when he was its object: "a sort of description of the splendid, magical talent deployed" in the work he is examining, while avoiding too personal a point of view, and basing himself on detailed information. One notices too the spontaneous generosity of his praise. Though convinced that there is no "Truth in Art," Satie admits and understands the differences between personalities. "Strawinsky is a magnificent bird," he said, for example, "and I am a fish..."

76. Satie here refers to the difference of thirteen days between the Julian and the Gregorian calendar. Since this difference grows by one

day a century, Strawinsky himself pointed out that it would mean that in 23,360 centuries it would make him born "after" his grandson.

77. Ernest Ansermet conducted the first performance of *Parade*, in 1917.

78. From the manuscript, on eleven sheets written on one side, numbered 1 to 11, in a school exercise book.

Proposed to Sybil Harris for *Vanity Fair*, with no result. This article gave Satie the opportunity to sum up a friendship that was very important to him, but also very painful as it ended in a quarrel.

79. Novel by George Sand, which recalls the affair between Haydn and Porpora, while, as in so many of her works, generally setting the demands of love in opposition to those of society.

80. From a manuscript on pages of a school exercise book, written on one side only, dated "4th Feb. 1918." (Private collection.)

The text of a lecture given at the Theatre du Vieux Colombier, on 5th Feb. 1918, at the time when Satie's friends were working to have his sentence lifted after he was condemned to eight days in prison and a one thousand francs fine, for having offended a critic (see note 53).

As in all the lectures he gave in the latter part of his life, Satie was careful to mark with a variable number of dots, the rhetorical effects he intended.

81. Translator's note. Buddha is written *Bouddha* in French, and the pronunciation is very similar to *boudin*, a blood sausage equivalent to the English black pudding, and a cheeky way of referring to the rounder and stupider among us.

82. Translator's note. *Mérite agricole* is the name of a medal given to prize-winning farmers by the state in France.

83. From a manuscript written on thirteen sheets of an exercise book, which also contains the text of his talk on Music and Animals. Undated (1921). (The University of Harvard, Cambridge, Mass., The Houghton Library, Satie Manuscripts.)

84. It is ironic to see Satie here advising people not to pay the music teacher too much, when we know piano lessons were one of his few sources of income.

85. From a manuscript written out on eleven sheets on one side only of an exercise book. Dated "Brussels, 15th March 1924 - Antwerp 21st March 1924". (Private collection.)

This text, written for his last tour of Belgium, at the invitation of the critic Paul Collaer, artistic director of the

Quartet Pro Arte, was Satie's very last lecture and may be considered his musical testament.

86. For Vuillermoz and Laloy see note 47 above. Boris de Schloezer (1881-1969) was a Russian musicologist, and the first to write about the "Satie case" being more a question of personality than music. Satie has added a "t" to make his name more "boche."

87. *L'Avenir d'Arcueil-Cachan*, "Organ of the Radical and Radical-Socialist Party," October 1909-June 1910, in a column called *La Quinzaine des Sociétés*.

Even without the evidence of Pierre-Daniel Templier, Satie's first biographer and the son of this paper's editor, the architect Pierre-Alexandre Templier, the inimitable style of these advertisements would be enough to attribute them to our composer.

At the turn of the century, artists and poets were fascinated by advertising. Blaise Cendrars considered it one of the "seven wonders of the modern world," along with "Satie's music which you listen to without your head between your hands".

88. The "apaches" were turn of the century street-thieves operating in the poorer parts of Paris where the bourgeois liked to come and "live it rough." Satie carried a hammer in his pocket for protection on his late-night walks from Paris back to Arcueil; it is not recorded whether he ever had to use it.

Ravel's friends, including poet Leon-Paul fargue and pianist Ricardo Viñes, called their band of music-lovers, the "Apaches."

89. The texts in this section are from manuscript notes in the margins of Erik Satie's music notebooks, or more rarely on loose sheets of paper, from about 1890 up to 1924. (Harvard University, the Houghton Library, Satie Manuscripts, Bibliothèque Nationale de France, Département de la Musique, Fonds Erik Satie & Private collections.)

I have arranged these various observations — whether commentaries, impressions, or fairy stories — which Satie was in the habit of jotting down in the minuscule music-paper notebooks he always carried in his pocket, in the chronological order suggested by the presence of known musical works in the same notebook.

These reflections were implicitly addressed only to himself. He did, however, publish some from time to time in the numerous avant-garde reviews which asked him to contribute in the early twenties. He usually included them in an itinerant column (by which I mean wandering from one review to another), called *A Mammal's Notebooks (extracts)*. Those published in the composer's lifetime have an explanatory note.

90. Published in *Le Coq*, 1, May 1920.

91. *Ibid*.

92. Published in *Le Coq*, 2, June 1920

93. Published in *Le Coq*, 3, July/August-September 1920.

94. Published in *Le Pilhaou-Thibaou*, illustrated supplement to *391*, 10 July 1921. *"J'aimerais jouer avec un piano qui aurait une grosse queue."* A grand piano is a *"piano à queue."* *Queue* also means a prick in French.

95. *Ibid. "Ce n'est pas beau de parler du noeud de la question."* *Noeud* (knot) also means the glans of the penis.

96. Published under the title *Cahiers d'un Mammifère (extraits)* in *L'Esprit Nouveau*, II, 7, April 1921, p. 833-834.

97. *Ibid*.

98. *Ibid*.

99. Published under the title *Cahiers d'un Mammifère (extraits de malt)* in *Crèation*, 3, February 1929, p. 3.

100. Published under the title *Cahiers d'un Mammifère (extraits)* in *391*, 18, July 1924, p. 2.

101. After Erik Satie's death four thousand little cards were found in his room in Arcueil, amid an indescribable mess, carefully stored in cigar boxes, each describing in neat calligraphy, in the form of small advertisements, elements of a looking-glass world. About one hundred and fifty of these cards have survived. (Same sources as those of note 89 above.)

102. French pun on *Pin blanc* (white pine) and *Pain blanc* (*"manger du pain blanc"* means "to live it up").

103. Untranslatable pun on *Pot rouge* (red pot) and *Peau rouge* (redskin).

IV. CATALOGUE OF ERIK SATIE'S MUSICAL & LITERARY
WORKS, WITH COMMENTS BY THE SAME GENTLEMAN

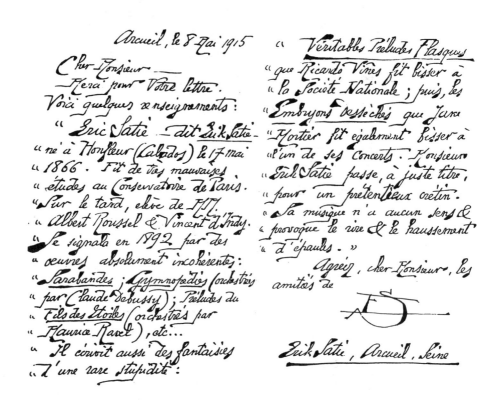

Arcueil, 8th May 1915

Dear Sir,[1]

    Thank you for your letter. Herewith a few details:

    "Eric Satie — known as Erik Satie — born in Honfleur (Calvados) the 17th May 1866. Thoroughly bad student at the Conservatoire de Paris. Late in the day, pupil of MM. Albert Roussel & Vincent d'Indy. Attracted attention in 1892 with some completely incoherent works: Sarabands; Gymnopédies *(orchestrated by Claude Debussy);* Preludes to the Son of the Stars *(orchestrated by Maurice Ravel), etc.. He also wrote some remarkably stupid fantasies:* Genuine Flabby Preludes, *which were encored by Ricardo Viñes at the Société Nationale; then the* Dried Embryos *which also won Jane Mortier an encore at one of her concerts. Monsieur Erik Satie is, quite rightly, taken for a pretentious cretin. His music is senseless & makes people laugh & shrug their shoulders."*

    Agréez, cher Monsieur, les amitiés de

ES

Erik Satie, Arcueil, Seine

---

1. Unpublished letter to Paul Viardot, who was compiling a "Dictionary of Musicians."

An English translation of all titles is provided in curved brackets, except where unnecessary, where Satie's own title includes an explanation in brackets, "curly" brackets have been employed. Titles, or parts thereof, in square brackets are those given by the publishers of posthumous publications. Dates given correspond to the earliest known documentation (publication, concert programme, bulletin of the Society of Authors, letters, etc.) for the title in question. Dates given in inverted commas appear on the original manuscripts. Dates in square brackets, sometimes with a question mark, have been deduced from cross-references.

1884

"9th September" *Allegro*, for piano.

1887

17th March *Valse-Ballet Op. 62* (Waltz-Ballet Op. 62), for piano.

April *Elégie* (Elegy), words by J.P. Contamine de Latour, for voice and piano.

June-July *Trois Mélodies, Op. 20* (Three Melodies, Op. 20), poem by J.P. Contamine de Latour, for voice and piano.

I. *Les Anges* (Angels). II. *Les Fleurs* (Flowers). III. *Sylvie.*

28th July *Fantaisie-Valse* (Fantasy-Waltz), for piano.

"September" *Sarabande, Ière, IIe, IIIe* (Saraband, Ist, IInd, IIIrd), with epigraph by J.P. Contamine de Latour, for piano.

Lively Saraband.[2]

1888

[April?] *Chanson, Op.52* (Song, Op. 52), poem by J.P. Contamine de Latour, for voice and piano.

In thisse Lodgeing be Lette Ye very Comely and most gratious Melodyes of Messire Erik Satie, high Master in ye Arte of Musick, player of ye Organ in ye Sainte Chapelle of Our Lord ye King, with ye verses of Messire I. P. Contamine de Latour, Scrivener of high Phantasie, Poet, Maker of Tales, Stories, Chronicles, and many other prettye things.[3]

---

2. The title first given on the original manuscript. Private collection.
3. Satie attached this notice to his door (c.1892?) to advertise his creations.

"February to 2nd April"	*Gymnopédie Ist, IInd, IIIrd*, for piano.

> *Just published at 66 Bd. Magenta, the Third* Gymnopédie *by Erik Satie. We cannot recommend too highly to music-lovers at large this deeply artistic work which is rightly described as one of the finest of the age into which this poor gentleman was born.*[4]

October to December	Texts either unsigned, or signed as "Virginie Lebeau," for the journals *Le Chat Noir* and *La Lanterne Japonaise*.

1889

[January]	*Ogives I, II, III, IV*, for piano.

> *At last! Lovers of gay music can indulge to their heart's content.*
> *The indefatigable Erik Satie, the sphinx-man, the wooden-headed composer, has announced the appearance of a new musical work, of which he speaks for the moment as highly as can be.*
> *It is a suite of melodies conceived in the mystico-liturgical style idolised by the composer, with the evocative title of:* Ogives.
> *We wish Erik Satie a similar success to that of his Third* Gymnopédie, *currently under everyone's piano.*
> *On sale at 66 Boulevard Magenta.*[5]

January to March	Unsigned texts for *Le Chat Noir* and texts signed "Virginie Lebeau" for *La Lanterne Japonaise*.
"8th July"	[*Fifth*] *Gnossienne*, for piano.

1890

"1890"	*Gnossienne*, No. 3, for piano.

1891

"20th January"	[*Première Pensée Rose+Croix*] [First Rosicrucian Thought], for piano.
"22nd January"	[*Fourth*] *Gnossienne*, for piano.
"28th October"	*Leitmotiv du Panthée* (Leitmotiv for Panthea), Xth ethopoeia from the Sâr Péladan's *Latin Decadence*, for piano.
"2nd November"	*Salut Drapeau* (Hail to the Flag), prose by the Sâr Péladan, an excerpt from

---

4. *Le Chat Noir*, VII, N. 358, 24 Nov. 1888.
5. *Le Chat Noir*, VIII, N. 369, 9 Feb. 1889.

✝✝ Dédicace :

Sans préjudice des pratiques des grands imprécateurs
Mes cousins, J'offre cette œuvre à Mes pairs.
Par ainsi, et pour la précédence des exemples, Je ne demande
point l'exaltation. J'appelle sur Mes convices
la miséricorde du Père, créateur des choses visibles et
invisibles ; la protection de la
Mère Auguste du Rédempteur, Reine des Anges ;
comme les prières du chœur
glorieux des Apôtres et des Saints Ordres des
Esprits bienheureux.
Que la juste inflammation de Dieu
écrase les superbes et les indécents !

Erik Satie ✝✝

his *The Prince of Byzantium*, for voice and piano.

1892

10th March

Sonneries de la Rose+Croix (Trumpet call for the Rosy Cross), for piano (and harp and trumpets?).

    I. *Air de l'Ordre* (Air for the Order). II. *Air du Grand Maître* (Air for the Grand Master). III. *Air du Grand Prieur* (Air for the Grand Prior).

    The Order bans all virtuosity, and considers that the instrumentalist, whosoever it be, should aspire to be only the ecstatic celebrant of masterpieces.[6]

17th March

Le Fils des Etoiles (The Son of the Stars), a Chaldean pastoral (*"wagnérie"*) by the Sâr Péladan, for piano (and harp and flutes?).

    Three Preludes: I. *La Vocation* (Vocation). II. *L'Initiation* (Initiation). III. *L'Incantation* (Incantation).

    Dedicatory. (See previous page)
Without prejudice to My cousins the great Imprecators, I offer this work to My Peers. For this cause, and for the sake of precedent in example, I request not exaltation.

    I ask for the mercy of the Father upon those that share my table, the Father that is creator of all that is visible and invisible; and the protection of the August Mother of the redeemer, Queen of the Angels, likewise the prayers of the glorious choir of the Apostles and the Holy Orders of the blessed Spirits.

    May the righteous flame of God crush the Overweening and the Indecent! [7]

12th June

Prélude du "Nazaréen" (Prelude to "The Nazarene") historical drama by Henri Mazel, for piano.

?

Prélude d'Eginhard (Prelude to Eginhard), for piano.

"12th August"

Open letter to *Gil Blas*.

[Summer?]

Fête donnée par des chevaliers normands en l'honneur d'une jeune démoiselle {XIe siècle}; (Feast given by Norman knights in honour of a young damsel {XIth Century}).

"17th November"

Uspud, "Christian ballet in three acts by J.P. Contamine de Latour, sacred music by Erik Satie," for piano (or harmonium?).

---

6. Note in the margin of the poster/programme for the *First Soirée of the Rose + Croix*, 17 [19] Nov. 1892.

7. *Le Fils des Etoiles*, "Chaldean Wagnery" by the Sâr Péladan, preludes, E. Baudoux, Paris, 1896, frontispiece.

This work was completed to our great joy the 72nd of Works of Hermetic Contemplation, as Evening was coming on.[8]

[24th December?]   *Noël* [Carol], words by Vincent Hyspa, for harmonium (lost).

1893

"21st -23rd March"   *Danses Gothiques* (Gothic Dances), for piano.

         1. *A l'occasion d'une grande peine* (At a Moment of Great Suffering).
2. *Dans laquelle les Pères de la Très Véritable et Très Sainte Eglise sont invoqués* (In which the Fathers of the most True and Holy Church are Invoked).
3. *En faveur d'un Malheureux* (On Behalf of a Poor Wretch). 4. *A propos de Saint Bernard et de Sainte Lucie* (Talking of Saint Bernard and Saint Lucia).
5. *Pour les pauvres trépassés* (For the Poor Departed). 6. *Où il est question du pardon des injures reçues* (In Which we are Concerned with Forgiveness for Insults Received). 7. *Par pitié pour les ivrognes, honteux, débauchés, imparfaits, désagréables & faussaires en tous genres* (Out of Pity for Those that are Drunkards, Shameful, Debauched, Imperfect, Unpleasant, & Forgers of all Sorts). 8. *En le haut honneur du vénéré Saint Michel, le gracieux Archange* (In High Honour of the Blessed Saint Michael, Gracious Archangel). 9. *Après avoir obtenu la remise de ses fautes* (After Obtaining the Remission of one's Sins).

     Choristic Cultifications and Coadunations.
     Novena for the greater calm and firm tranquillity of my soul.[9]

"2nd April"   *Bonjour Biqui* (Good Morning Biqui), words by Erik Satie, for voice and piano, dedicated to Suzanne Valadon.

[April]   *Vexations* (Vexations), for piano.

     To play this motif 840 times in succession, one would do well to prepare oneself beforehand, in the deepest silence, with serious immobilities.[10]

June   *Grande Messe de l'Eglise métropolitaine d'Art,* (High Mass of the Metropolitan Church of Art), for organ.

"15th July"   *Modéré* (At a Gentle Pace), for piano (or organ?).

"15th October"   *Epître de Erik Satie Première aux Artistes catholiques et à tous les Chrétiens,*

---

8. *Uspud,* manuscript (first version) 17 Nov. 1892. Private collection.
9. Note in the margin of the original manuscript, Bibliothèque Nationale de France Département de la musique (BNF-MUS.), MS 10048.
10. At the head of the manuscript. Archives de la Fondation Erik Satie.

(First Epistle of Erik Satie to Catholic Artists and to all Christians), foundation charter of the Metropolitan Church of Art of Jesus Leader.

1894

March

Prélude de "la Porte Héroique du Ciel" (Prelude to "The Heroic Gate of Heaven"), esoteric drama by Jules Bois, for piano.

> *I wrote this* Prelude *in 1894, for the work by M. Jules Bois.*
> *M. Roland Manuel asked me in 1911 for authorisation to orchestrate this corner of my life.*
> *That is the simple story of a little prelude; a little prelude worked in ivory like a tapestry of sound, a little prelude full of mystical sweetness, a little prelude full of ecstatic joy, a little prelude full of intimate goodness.*
> *The form of it is naive and chaste; its harmonies are meditative and white, and follow the so respectable and touching conventions rightly established by our August Predecessors, the Venerated Masters of Antiphony, which is Supreme, Unique, Impeccable, Triumphant, Anonymous, Fascinating and Phenomenal.*[11]

1895

January

Commune qui mundi nefas, extract from the *Messe des Pauvres* (Mass for the Poor), for organ.

> *This mass is not a diversion offered to the faithful; it has as its purpose to increase the intensity of their prayers.*[12]

March

Intende Votis, for organ.

"May"

Cartulaire (monthly publication of the Metropolitan Church of Art of Jesus Leader), No. 1.

"June"

Cartulaire, No. 2.

June

Prière des Orgues de la Messe des Pauvres (Organ Prayer from the Mass for the Poor).

---

11. *Le Guide du Concert*, III, 35, 1 June 1912.
12. Conrad Satie (or is this Erik Satie?), *Erik Satie*, in *Le Coeur*, II, 10, June 1895.

1897

"January"   [*Sixth*] *Gnossienne.*

March   *Airs à faire fuir* (Airs to make flee), I, II, III, for piano.

March   *Danses de travers* (Cock-eyed dances), I, II, III, for piano (published in 1912, with the *Airs to make flee* in the collection called *Pièces Froides* (Cold pieces)).

?   *Je te veux* (I Want You), words by Henry Pacory, for voice and piano, or orchestra.

1899

May-July   *Jack in the Box*, pantomime in two acts by Jules Dépaquit, for piano.

> I. *Prélude* (Prelude). II. *Entr'acte* (Interval). III. *Finale.*

> *This piece of horseplay makes me feel a little better and gives me the chance to pull faces at the nasty men that populate this world.*[13]

September   *Un Dîner à l'Elysée* (Dinner at the Elysée Palace), words by Vincent Hyspa, for voice and piano.

?   *Le Veuf* (The Widower), words by Vincent Hyspa, for voice and piano.

1900

"18th April"   *Prélude de "La Mort de M. Mouche"* (Prelude to "The Death of Mr. Fly"), play by J.P. Contamine de Latour, for piano.

?   *Les Musiciens de Montmartre* (The Musicians of Montmartre), written for the *Guide de l'Etranger à Montmartre.*

"5th August"   *Verset laïque & somptueux* (Sumptuous lay verse), for piano.

?   *Geneviève de Brabant*, play in three acts, by Lord Cheminot (Contamine

---

13. Letter to Conrad Satie, 4 July 1899, cf. O. Volta, 1989, p. 79.

de Latour) in verse and prose, for voice and piano.

1901

"March"   *The Dreamy Fish,* "music for a story by Lord Cheminot," for piano.

?   *Le Boeuf Angora — The Angora Ox,* "music to a story by Lord Cheminot," for orchestra.

1902

November   *Poudre d'Or* (Gold Powder), waltz, for piano or orchestra.

November   *Tendrement* (Tenderly), "singing waltz," words by Vincent Hyspa, for voice and piano.

I am writing crude rubbish and it is not good for me.[14]

1903

August-November   *Trois Morceaux en forme de poire avec une Manière de Commencement, une Prolongation du même et un En Plus, suivi d'une Redite* (Three Pieces in the Form of a Pear with a Manner of a Beginning, a Prolongation thereof, Followed by an In Addition, and then a To Say It Again), for piano duet.

Monsieur Erik Satie is wild about this latest creation of his wit. He talks about it a lot, and speaks very highly of it.
He thinks it is better than anything that has been written to this day. He may be wrong but one should not tell him so; he would not believe it.[15]

Recommendation
I am at a prestigious turning-point in the History of My Life.
In this work I express My decent, natural astonishment.
Believe me in spite of all you have heard.
Do not play with the unknown amulets of your ephemeral penetration; make holy your cherished verbal blisters: God will pardon you, if he so desires, from the honourable centre of conjunctive Eternity where all is known in solemnity by persuasion.
The Definite cannot freeze; the Ardent wipes itself away, the Choleric has no reason to be.
I cannot promise any better for having multiplied myself tenfold provisionally, though in the face of all caution.

---

14. Letter to Conrad Satie, 1903.
15. Letter to Claude Debussy, 17 August 1903, cf. O. Volta, 1989, p. 146.

Is that not all?
I tell myself it is.[16]

What a drag my old music is!
What rubbish, if I may say so![17]

1904

January   *Petit Recueil des Fêtes* (Little Feast Day Collection), words by Vincent Hyspa, for voice and piano.
       I. *Le Picador est mort* (The Picador is dead). II. *Sorcière* (Witch). III. *Enfant-martyre* (Child-martyr). IV. *Air fantôme* (Phantom Air).

Spring   *J'avais un ami* (I Had a Friend), words by unknown author, for voice and piano.

20th May   *La Diva de "L'Empire,"* singing march, American intermezzo, words by Dominique Bonnaud and Numa Blès, for voice and piano, or orchestra.

19th October   *Le "Piccadilly,"* march, for voice and piano or string quintet.

1905

18th August   *Imperial Oxford*, song without words, for piano.

18th August   *Légende californienne* (Californian Legend), song without words, for piano.

1906

11th January   *Allons-y Chochotte* (Let's Go, Chochotte), words by D. Durante, for voice and piano.

March   *Chez le Docteur* (At the Doctor's), words by Vincent Hyspa, for voice and piano.

March   *L'Omnibus-automobile* (The Motorised Omnibus), words by Vincent Hyspa, for voice and piano.

26th April   *Pousse l'Amour* (Nudge Love), play by Jean Kolb and Maurice de Féraudy, for piano (lost).

"July"   *Passacaille* (Passacaglia), for piano.

"21st October"   *Prélude en Tapisserie* (Tapestry Prelude), for piano.

---

16. In the margin of the original manuscript, dated "6th November 1903." Bibliothèque-Musée de l'Opéra de Paris, Rés. 218.
17. Letter to Ricardo Viñes, 19 April 1916, cf. O. Volta, 1989, p.108.

?	*Chanson {médiévale}* ({Medieval} Song), poem by Catulle Mendès, for voice and piano.

1907

August	*{Nouvelles} Pièces froides* ({Further} Cold Pieces), "suite for a dog," for piano. I. *Sur un Mur* (On a Wall). II. *Sur un Arbre* (On a Tree). III. *Sur un Pont* (On a Bridge).

1908

January	*Réception à Rambouillet* (Reception at Rambouillet), words by Vincent Hyspa, for voice and piano.
January	*Clémenceau à Marienbad* (Clémenceau at Marienbad), words by Vincent Hyspa, for voice and piano.
?	*Les Oiseaux* (The Birds), words by Vincent Hyspa?, for voice and piano.[18]
"29th January"	*Fâcheux Exemple* (Annoying Example), for piano.
"12th February"	*Désespoir agréable* (Pleasant Despair), for piano.
?	*Petite Sonate* (Little Sonata), for piano.
"1st August"	*Choral & Fugue*, for piano duet.

> *After three years of hard labour, here I am in 1908 with a diploma in my hand which bestows on me the title of contrapuntalist.*
> *Proud of my learning, I set out to compose.*
> *My first work in this style is Choral & Fugue for piano duet.*
> *I have certainly been yelled at in my poor life, but never have I been so looked down on. What had I been up to with d'Indy?*
> *I had written pieces before with such rich charm!*
> *And now?*
> *What a drag! What a bore!*[19]

1909

?	*Deux Choses* (Two Things), for piano. I. *Effronterie {Elégie commercial}* (Effrontery {Commercial elegy}).

---

18 *Réception à Rambouillet* and *Clémenceau à Marienbad*, identified in the repertoire of Vincent Hyspa by Steven Moore Whiting, were published with *Les Oiseaux*, as *Trois Mélodies sans paroles*, Salabert, Paris, 1978.

19. Letter to Conrad Satie, 17 Jan. 1911, cf. O. Volta, 1989, p. 23-24.

II. *Poésie* (Poem).

? *Profondeur {Bévue indiscrète, ou le Viz ir autrichien}* (Depth {Indiscreet blunder, or the Austrian Vizir}), for piano.

? *Menuet Basque* (Basque Minuet), for piano.

? *Le Conteur magique* (The Magic Storyteller), for piano.

? *Songe-Creux* (Hollow-Dream), for piano.

? *Le Prisonnier Maussade* (The Sullen Prisoner), for piano.

? *Le Grand Singe* (The Big Monkey), for piano.

September *Le Dîner de Pierrot* (Pierrot's Dinner), play by Bertrand Millanvoye?, for piano (lost).

October - December Unsigned advertisements for the *Avenir d'Arcueil-Cachan*.

October *La Chemise* (The Shirt), words by Jules Dépaquit, for voice and piano.

1911

to November *En Habit de Cheval* (In Horse Dress), for piano duet, or orchestra.
I. *Choral* (Chorale). II. *Fugue litanique* (Litany fugue). III. *Autre Choral* (Another Chorale). IV. *Fugue de Papier* (Paper Fugue).

Fantasy explained: I gave to two chorales and two fugues the title In Horse Dress.
Well-meaning people have often asked me to be kind enough to give them details of this equestrian costume.
What exactly does it consist of? A jacket? A riding-coat? Boots, or jodhpurs with foot-straps?
Is the rider wearing a hat? or a cap? or a beret? What is his cravat like?
I have to say I meant to refer to one of the horse's own garments... For example: two poles attached to a four-wheel carriage...[20]

---

20. Note transcribed c. 1930 by P.-D. Templier from a ms. held by Conrad Satie, now lost.

1912

?	*Deux Préludes pour un chien* (Two Preludes for a Dog), for piano.
February	*Ambroise Thomas*, text for *L'Oeil de Veau*.
15th April	*Mémoires d'un Amnésique: Ce que je suis* (Memoirs of an Amnesic: What I Am), for the *Revue musicale S.I.M.*
May-June	*Observations d'un Imbécile: Juste Remarque* (Observations of an Idiot: Valid Point), text for *L'Oeil de Veau*.
July	*Préludes Flasques {pour un chien}* (Flabby Preludes {for a dog}), for piano. I. *Voix d'intérieur* (Inner voice). II. *Idylle cynique* (Cynical Idyll). III. *Chanson canine* (Canine Song). IV. *Sous la futaille* (Beneath the Barrel).[21]
July-August	*Mémoires d'un Amnésique: Parfaite Entourage* (Perfect Entourage), for the *Revue musicale S.I.M.*
"12th to 23rd August"	*Véritables Préludes flasques {pour un chien}* (Genuine Flabby Preludes {for a Dog}), for piano. I. *Sévère Reprimande* (Severe Reprimand). II. *Seul à la maison* (Alone in the House). III. *On Joue* (Let us Play).

> *They were composed for a dog... They are dedicated to that animal.*
> *They are three piano pieces, short and without pretention.*
> *In them I indulge in the sweet joys of fantasy.*
>
> *Those that do not understand me are requested, by me, to observe the most respectful silence and to show an attitude wholly of submission and inferiority. That is their proper role.*[22]

"October"	*Aperçus désagréables* [23] (Unpleasant Glimpses), for piano duet. I. *Pastorale*. II. *Choral*. III. *Fugue*.

> *The lovely, limpid* Unpleasant Glimpses *are in the most elevated style and clearly explain why this subtle composer has the right to say: "Before writing a work, I walk around it several times, accompanied by myself."*[24]

---

21. This title (according to Robert Orledge, 1990, p. 296), was withdrawn by Satie at Debussy's request, and replaced in the posthumous edition (Max Eschig, 1967) by the indication "With Camaraderie."
22. From manuscript notes collected by Pierre-Daniel Templier (cf. note 21 above), part of which were published in *Le Guide du Concert*, IV, 25, 29 March 1913.
23. This piece reuses the *Chorale & Fugue* of 1908, with the addition of a Pastorale.
24. From *Erik Satie*, by A.L., see *infra*. December 1913.

November

Mémoires d'un Amnésique: Mes trois Candidatures (Memoirs of an Amnesic: My Three Candidatures), for the *Revue musicale S.I.M.*

1913

January

Mémoires d'un Amnésique: Choses de Théâtre (Theatre Things), for the *Revue musicale S.I.M.*

February

Mémoires d'un Amnésique: La Journée du musicien (The Musician's Day), *ibid.*

March

Le Piège de Méduse (Medusa's Snare), "Lyrical comedy by Erik Satie with music for dancing by the same gentleman," for piano.

> *This is a play of pure fantasy... with no reality.*
> *A joke.*
> *Do not see it as anything else.*
> *The role of Baron Medusa is a sort of portrait... Even a portrait of me... a full length portrait of me.*[25]

"21st to 26th April"

Descriptions automatiques (Automatic Descriptions), for piano.
I. *Sur un Vaisseau* (On a Vessel). II. *Sur une Lanterne* (On a Lantern). III. *Sur un Casque* (On a Helmet).

> *I wrote these* Automatic Descriptions *on the occasion of my birthday.*
> *It is quite obvious that the Squashed, the Insignificant, and the Bloated will derive no pleasure from it.*
> *They can swallow their beards! They can dance on their own bellies!* [26]

"2nd June to 25th August"

Croquis & Agaceries d'un gros Bonhomme en bois (Sketches and Teases by a Big Wooden Dummy), for piano.
I. *Tyrolienne Turque* (Turkish Tyrolienne). II. *Danse maigre {à la manière de ces Messieurs}* (Meagre Dance {in the Style of Those Gentlemen}). III. *Españana.*

---

25. Manuscript notes transcribed by P-D Templier (cf. note 20 above).
26. From *Erik Satie*, by A.L. 1913.

"30th June to 4th July" *Embryons desséchés* (Dried Embryos), for piano.
I. *d'Holothurie* (Of Holothuria). II. *d'Edriophthalma* (Of Edriophthalma). III. *de Podophthalma* (Of Podophthalma).

This work is utterly incomprehensible, even to me.
Its singular profundity continually astonishes me.
I wrote it in spite of myself, at the urging of Destiny.
Was I perhaps trying to create humour?
That would not surprise me and would be rather my style.
All the same I shall have no sympathy for people who make light of it.
They stand warned.[27]

"2nd August" *San Bernardo*, for piano.

"23rd August to 5th September" *Chapitres tournés en tous sens* (Chapters Turned this Way and That), for piano.
I. *Celle qui parle trop* (She who Talks too Much). II *Le Porteur de grosses Pierres* (The Man Who Carries Big Stones). III. *Regret des Enfermés {Jonas et Latude}* (The Prisoners' Lament {Jonah and Latude}).

The Chapters Turned this Way and That *were fashioned from a spoilsport grin.*
They are a sort of easy-going figurative piece detached from the Genuine Flabby Preludes, *the* Automatic Descriptions *and the* Dried Embryos. *I request that they be listened to sip by sip, without rushing.*
May Modesty settle on the mouldering shoulders of the Hunched up and Submerged! They shall not be embellished with my friendship!
It is an adornment which is not for them.[28]

"9th to 17th September" *Vieux Sequins & Vieilles Cuirasses* (Old Sequins & Old Breastplates), for piano.
I. *Chez le Marchand d'Or {Venise, XIIIe siècle}* (At the Gold-Merchant's {Venice, XIIIth Century}). II. *Danse cuirassée {période grecque}* (Dance in Armour {Greek period}). III. *La défaite des Cimbres {Cauchemar}* (Defeat of the Cimbrians {Nightmare}).

November? [*Trois nouvelles Enfantines*] [Three New Children's Pieces], for piano.
I. *Le Vilain petit Vaurien* (Nasty Little Good-for-nothing). II. [*Berceuse*] (Lullaby). III. *La gentille toute petite Fille* (The Sweet Little Tiny Girl).

"September" *L'Enfance de Ko-Quo {Recommandations maternelles}* (Ko-Quo's Childhood {Motherly Advice}), for piano.
I. *Ne bois pas ton chocolat avec tes doigts* (Do not drink your chocolate with

27. Manuscript notes transcribed by P.-D. Templier, cf. note 20.
28. *Le Guide du Concert*, V, 14, 10 Jan. 1914.

your fingers). II. *Ne souffle pas dans tes oreilles* (Do not blow in your ears). III. *Ne mets pas ta tête sous ton bras* (Do not put your head under your arm).

These pieces were written with the aim of preparing children for the sound patterns of modern music.

They have won me congratulations from the Shah of Persia and the King of Yvetot.[29]

"October"

Menus Propos enfantins (Childish Prattle), for piano.
I. *Le Chant guerrier du Roi des Haricots* (The King of the Beans' War Song). II. *Ce que dit la Princesse des Tulipes* (What the Tulip Princess Said). III. *Valse du Chocolat aux Amandes* (The Almond Chocolate Waltz).

"October"

Enfantillages pittoresques (Colourful Childish Pursuits), for piano.
I. *Petit Prélude à la Journée* (Little Prelude to the Day). II. *Berceuse* (Lullaby). III. *Marche du grand Escalier* (Steps of the Grand Staircase).

"October"

Peccadilles importunes (Tiresome Peccadilloes), for piano.
I. *Etre jaloux de son camarade qui a une grosse tête* (Being Jealous of your Friend Who Has Got a Big Head). II. *Lui manger sa tartine* (Eating his Bread and Butter). III. *Profiter de ce qu'il a des cors aux pieds pour lui prendre son cerceau* (Taking Advantage of the Fact he has Corns on his Feet to Pinch his Hoop).

"November"

Les Pantins Dansent (The Puppets Dance), dance to a poem by Valentine de Saint-Point, for piano, or orchestra.

December

Erik Satie, text signed "A.L." [Alfred Leslie, his middle names] for the cata-catalogue of Agence E. Demets.

1914

"17th to 30th January"

Choses vues à droite et à gauche {sans lunettes} (Things seen to left and right {without glasses}), for violin and piano.
I. *Choral hypocrite* (Hypocritical Chorale). II. *Fugue à tâtons* (Fumbling Fugue). III. *Fantaisie musculaire* (Muscular Fantasy).

---

29. In the margin of the manuscript. Private collection.

My chorales are the equal of Bach's, with the difference that they are rarer and less pretentious.[30]

1st February

Mémoires d'un Amnésique: L'Intelligence et la Musicalité chez les Animaux (Intelligence and Musicality Among Animals), for the *Revue musicale S.I.M.*

May

Globules ennuyeaux (Bothersome Globs), for piano.
    I. *Regard* (The Look in her Eyes). II. *Superficies* (Surface). III. *Canalisation* (Piping). Unfinished work.

?

Souvenirs fadasses (Insipid Memories), for piano.
    I. *Barbouillage* (Scrawl). II. *Poil* (Hair). III. *Recrudescence.* Unfinished work

?

Rêverie sur un plat (Reverie on a Dish), for piano.

"14th March to 20th May"

Sports & Divertissements (Sports & Recreations), drawings by Charles Martin, for piano.
    I. *Choral inappétissant* (Unappetising Chorale). II. *La Balançoire* (The Swing). III. *La Chasse* (Hunting). IV. *La Comédie italienne* (Italian Comedy). V. *Le Réveil de la Mariée* (The Bride's Reveille). VI. *Colin-Maillard* (Blind Man's Buff). VII. *La Pêche* (Fishing). VIII. *Le Yachting* (Yachting). IX. *Le Bain de mer* (Bathing). X. *Le Carnaval* (Carnival). XI. *Le Golf* (Golf). XII. *La Pieuvre* (The Octopus). XIII. *Les Courses* (The Races). XIV. *Les Quatre Coins* (Puss in the Corner). XV. *Le Pique-nique* (The Picnic). XVI. *Le Water-Chute* (The Water Chute). XVII. *Le Tango perpétuel* (Non-stop Tango). XVIII. *Le Traîneau* (The Sledge). XIX. *Le Flirt* (Flirting). XX. *Le Feu d'Artifice* (Fireworks). XXI. *Le Tennis* (Tennis).

This publication is made up of two artistic elements: drawing and music.
The drawing part is composed of lines — spirited lines; the musical part is represented by dots — black dots. These two parts brought together — in a single volume — form a whole: an album.
I recommend browsing through this book with a friendly, smiling finger for it is a work of fantasy. It should not be seen as anything else.
For the "Shrivelled" and the "Dimwits," I have written a suitably ponderous chorale.
This chorale is a sort of bitter preamble, a kind of austere, unfrivolous introduction. I have put into it all I know about Ennui.
I dedicate this chorale to those who do not like me.[31]

---

30. In the margin of the ms. Bibliothèque-Musée de l'Opéra de Paris, Rés. 219 (Jan. 1914).
31. Preface to the musical album *Sports et Divertissements*, Lucien Vogel, Paris, [1923].

(June?)	*Un Acte* (An Act), scenario for a ballet.
"25th June to 3rd July"	*Heures séculaires et instantanées* (Instantaneous Centuries-old Hours), for piano.

    I. *Obstacles venimeux* (Venomous Obstacles). II. *Crepuscule matinal {de midi}* (Morning Twilight {at Midday}). III. *Affolements granitiques* (Haywire in Granite).

"21st to 23rd July"	*Les trois Valses distinguées du Précieux dégoûté* (Three Elegant Waltzes by a Squeamish Pansy), for piano.

    I. *Sa Taille* (His Waist). II. *Son binocle* (His Pince-Nez). III. *Ses jambes* (His legs).

"20th November to 2 December"	*Trois Poèmes d'Amour* (Three Love Poems), words by Erik Satie, for voice and piano.

    I. The Poet dares to make a discreet declaration to his lover, a pale avowal. She listens coldly, with pursed lips. III. The Poet here expresses all his devotion, all his reverence. He doubts his personal capacity and shows enormous anxiety. II. The Poet turns dizzy and seems mad with love. His heart bursts in his belly, his eyelids tremble like leaves.

    These poems are not concerned with love of Glory, love of Lucre, love of Commerce, or love of Geography.

    No, these poems are poems about love... of Love; they are simple happy pages in which can be seen all the tenderness of a virtuous man with very proper habits.

    You can listen to them without fear.

    They are three in number: the first has the title: Love Poem No. 1; *the title of the second one is slightly less glorious:* Love Poem No. 3; *while the third poem's title is yet more modest:* Love Poem No. 2.

    I shall sing them to you myself, on a single vocal chord, as was the practice in the olden days, at the Court of our good old kings in the XIIth... in the XIIth arrondissement.[32]

1915

"2nd April"	*Cinq Grimaces pour "le Songe d'une Nuit d'Eté"* (Five Grimaces for "A Midsummer Night's Dream"), comedy by William Shakespeare, for orchestra.

    I. *Préambule* (Preamble). II. *Coquecigrue*. III. *Fanfaronnade*. IV. *Chasse* (Hunt). V. *Pour Sortir {Retraite}* (The Way Out {Retreat}).

23rd August to 5th October	*Avant-Dernières Pensées* (Thoughts-Before-Last), for piano.

---

32. Manuscript notes in the margin of the roughs for the score, BNF-MUS, MS 9615 (1).

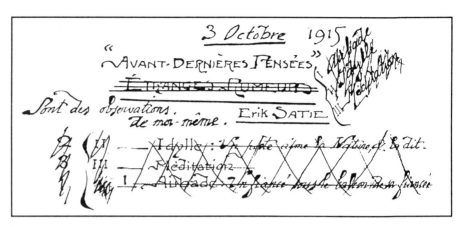

I. *Idylle* (Idyll). II. *Aubade*. III. *Méditation* (Meditation).

...are observations of myself
Idyll: *a Poet loves nature and says so.*
Aubade: *a fiancé below the balcony of his betrothed.*[33]

1916

"14th April" *Daphénéo,* words by M. God [Mimi Godebski], for voice and piano.

"14th April" *Le Chapelier* (The Hatter), words by René Chalupt, after *Alice in Wonderland*, for voice and piano.

> *[I am] the only Frenchman who understands English Humour and the only composer whose music understands* Alice.[34]

"26th May" *La Statue de Bronze* (The Bronze Statue), poem by Léon-Paul Fargue, for voice and piano.

> *Send me — immediately — something very* short *and awfully cynical.*[35]

2nd November *La Musique et les Animaux* (Music & Animals), lecture for Ecole Lucien, Flagny.

1917

8th-24th March *Embarquement pour Cythère* (Embarking for Cythaera), for violin and piano.

"2nd May" *A Tale,* text in *The Blind Man.*

May 1916 to April 1917 *Parade,* theme by Jean Cocteau, curtain, sets, costumes by Pablo Picasso,

---

33. In the margin of the manuscript sketches. Private collection.
34. Louise Varèse, *Varèse, a Looking-Glass Diary,* Davis-Poynter, London, 1973, p.161.
35. Letter to Léon-Paul Fargue, 16 May 1916. Private collection.

choreography by Leonid Massine. For Orchestra, or piano duet.

Prélude du Rideau rouge (Red Curtain Prelude), *Premier Manager* (First Manager). I. *Le Prestidigitateur chinois* (The Chinese Conjuror). II. *La Petite Fille Américaine* (The Little American Girl). III. *Les Acrobates* (The Acrobats). *Suprême Effort et Chute des Managers* (The Managers Try their Absolute Hardest then Collapse). *Suite au "Prélude du Rideau rouge"* (Suite to the "Red Curtain Prelude").

I have written this little Red Curtain Prelude.
It is a very inward-looking fugue exposition, very serious, & even quite a "drag," but short.
I like this slightly "pompier," fake naive style, completely "kono" as the "Jappos" say.[36]

I have written a background to various noises the librettist finds indispensable for giving the right atmosphere to his characters.[37]

July — *Sonatine Bureaucratique* (Bureaucratic Sonatina), for piano.
I. *Allegro.* II. *Andante.* III. *Vivache.*

Written to themes borrowed from Clementi.
A simple loan, that is all.
This should just be seen as a bit of whimsy — a teeny bit. Yes.
It has no intention of impugning the said Clementi's reputation and honour.[38]

[August] — *[Alibi]*, text for Roland Manuel.

1918

[February] — *Eloge des Critiques* (A Eulogy of Critics), talk introducing a concert by the *Nouveaux Jeunes* at the Théâtre du Vieux Colombier.

"18th February" — [Dispatch].

[March?] — *Carrelage phonique* (Phonic Tiling), furniture music for a small ensemble.

To be played at a lunch, or a marriage contract.[39]

---

36. Letter to Valentine Gros (later Hugo), 12 Dec. 1916. Taken from V. Hugo, *Souvenir de Parade*, collage, 1965. Archives de la Fondation Erik Satie.

37. Jean Cocteau, *Petite chronique de la collaboration de "Parade," Nord-Sud*, I, 4/5, June-July 1917.

38. Manuscript notes, cf. note 20.

39. In the margin of the manuscript. Northwestern University, Music Library, coll. John Cage, Evanston, Illinois.

[March?]

Tapisserie en fer forgé pour l'arrivée des invités {grande réception} (Wrought

Iron Tapestry for the Arrival of the Guests {Grand Reception}), furniture music for a small ensemble.

To be played in a lobby.[40]

"Furniture Music" for soirées, meetings, etc
What is "Furniture Music"? — a pleasure!
"Furniture Music" replaces:
"waltzes,"
"fantasias from opera," *etc.*
Make no mistake! It is something quite different!!!
No more "fake music": musical furniture!
"Furniture Music" completes the decor; It makes
  everything possible; It is worth its weight in
  Gold; It is new; It does not disturb your habits;
It is not tiring; It is French; It is unusable; It is not
  boring.
To take it up means doing better.
Listen without feeling awkward.
OFF THE HOOK OR MADE TO MEASURE.[41]

January 1917 to October 1918

Socrate (Socrates), symphonic drama based on Plato's *Dialogues* in Victor Cousin's translation, for voices and orchestra, or piano.

I. *Portrait de Socrate {le Banquet}* (Portrait of Socrates {The Symposium}). II. *Les Bords de l'Ilissus {Phèdre}* (The Banks of the Ilissus {Phaedrus}). III. *Mort de Socrate {Phédon}* (The Death of Socrates {Phaedo}).

Plato is wonderful to work with, very gentle and never intrusive: a dream, really![42]
In writing this work... I had no desire to add to the beauty of Plato's Dialogues: *this is simply an act of piety, an artist's reverie... a humble homage...*

---

40. *Ibid.*
41. From the original manuscript. Private collection.
42. Letter to Valentine Gros, 18 Jan. 1917, cf. O. Volta, 1989, p.154.

198

Aesthetically this work is dedicated to clarity; simplicity accompanies, directs it... That is all ... I desired nothing else.[43]

It is not Russian, of course. And it is not Persian, either, or Oriental. It is a return to classical simplicity, with a modern sensibility.
I owe this return — to good behaviour — to my "Cubist" friends.
Bless them![44]

1919

April

Parade: Choral & Final, for orchestra or piano duet.

I am not displeased with my three minutes of music for my dear Director. He had a good idea. The work will be improved.[45]

This old piece — Parade *— is not so bad considering its age. Three: that's old.*[46]

August to October

Trois Nocturnes (Three Nocturnes), for piano.

I have just finished a third Nocturne. *I dedicate it to you.*
The three of them together are not bad.
The first acts as a prelude. The second, shorter one, is very tender, very nocturnal. The third one — yours — is a dramatic nocturne, a little longer than the first.
The three together form a whole which I am very pleased with.[47]

11th October

Notes sur la musique moderne (Notes on Modern Music), article for *l'Humanité.*

October-November

Quatrième, Cinquième, Sixième Nocturne (Fourth, Fifth, Sixth Nocturne), for piano.

This is another expression of me.
What is it?
I am at a turning-point for my state of mind, and not enjoying myself.[48]

---

43. Manuscript notes for the introduction to the first performance of *Socrate* at the Princesse de Polignac's, 1918?

44. Letter to Henry Prunières, 3 April 1918, cf. O. Volta, 1989, p. 150-152.

45. Letter to Henri-Pierre Roché, 22 April 1919. The University of Texas, Austin, HRHRC.

46. Letter to H. P. Roché, (6 May 1919). *Ibid.*

47. Letter to Valentine Hugo, 24 Aug. 1919. Private collection.

48. Letter to Valentine Hugo, 21 Aug. 1919, *ibid.*

"November"	*Marche de Cocagne* (Cocagne March), for two trumpets in C.

1920

January — *Trois petites Pièces montées* (Three Little Tiered cakes), for orchestra or piano duet.
    I. *De l'Enfance de Pantagruel {Rêverie}* (The Childhood of Pantagruel {Reverie}). II. *Marche de Cocagne {Démarche}* (Cocagne March {Approach}). III. *Jeux de Gargantua {Coin de Polka}* (Gargantua's Games {Pinch of Polka}).

March — *Musique d'Ameublement* (Furniture Music), for the intervals of Max Jacob's play *Ruffian toujours, Truand jamais*, for piano duet, three clarinets, and trombone.

"Furniture Music" is fundamentally industrial.
It is habitual — common practice — to make music on occasions with which music has nothing to do "Waltzes," "Fantasias" from Operas, & other such things are played, which were written with a different aim.
We wish to establish a form of music designed to satisfy "utility" requirements. Art does not come into these requirements.
"Furniture Music" creates vibration; it has no other purpose; it fills the same role as light, warmth, and comfort in all its forms.
• "Furniture Music" advantageously replaces marches, polkas, tangos, gavottes, &c.
• Insist on "Furniture Music."
• No meetings, assemblies etc. without "Furniture Music."
• "Furniture Music" for lawyers, banks, etc...
• "Furniture Music" has no first name.
• No wedding should be without "Furniture Music."
• Do not enter a house which does not use "Furniture Music."
• A man who has not heard "Furniture Music" does not know happiness.
• Do not go to sleep without listening to "Furniture Music" or you will sleep badly.[49]

April–May — Aphorisms for *Le Coq*, no. 1.

"June" — *Premier Menuet* (First Minuet), for piano.
    Written when I was very young (fifty four).[50]

June — *Pas de Casernes* (No Barracks), text for *Le Coq*, 2.

---

49. Outline for an advertisement tract. Manuscript [1 March 1920]. Bibliothèque Historique de la Ville de Paris, *fonds* Jean Cocteau.
50. Letter to Marcelle Meyer, 27 Sept 1921.

200

July	*Ne confondons pas* (Don't let us be confused), text for *Le Coq*, 3.
August-October	*La belle Excentrique* (The Eccentric Beauty), "serious fantasy," for orchestra or piano duet.

    I. *Marche franco-lunaire* (Franco-lunar March) — *Grande Ritournelle* (Grand Ritornello). II. *Valse du "Mystérieux Baiser dans l'Oeil"* (Waltz of "The Mysterious Kiss on the Eye") — *Grande Ritournelle* (Grand Ritornello). III. *Cancan Grand-Mondain* (High Society Cancan).

*   The "Eccentric Beauty" is a Parisienne from Paris. She can vaguely get through a few steps of shimmy, but she remains Parisienne. I am very fond of negroes but once again our "Eccentric" is Parisian, she's not a negress.*[51]

"24 September to 25 November"	*Quatre petites Mélodies* (Four Little Melodies), for voice and piano.

    I. *Elégie "à la mémoire de Debussy"* (Elegy "to the memory of Debussy"), poem *[l'Isolement]* by Lamartine. II. *Danseuse* (Dancer), poem by Jean Cocteau. III. *Chanson,* (Song), words anonymous, XVIIIth century. IV. *Adieu,* poem *[Mouchoir]* by Raymond Radiguet.

1921

"3rd" and "31st" January	Aphorisms for *391*.

*   This feels to me very suitable and very artistic without seeming to.*[52]

?	*Rêverie de l'Enfance de Pantagruel* (Reverie on the Childhood of Pantagruel), for piano
17th February	*Les Enfants Musiciens* (Child Musicians), lecture for an "Evening for Young People" at the Salle des Etoiles.
April	*Cahiers d'un Mammifère (extraits)* (A Mammal's Notebooks (extracts)), for *L'Esprit Nouveau*.
11th April	*Conférence sur les "Six"* (Lecture on "Les Six") to introduce a concert by the Groupe des Six at the Galerie Georges Giroux in Brussels.
[April?]	*Le Piège de Méduse* (Medusa's Snare), orchestral version of the *Seven little tiny dances*.
"30th August"	*Sonnerie pour réveiller le bon gros Roi des Singes {lequel ne dort toujours que*

51. Letter to Caryathis (Elisabeth Toulemon, later Elise Jouhandeau), 12 May 1921. Private collections.

52. Letter to Francis Picabia, 3 Jan. 1921. Bibliothèque littéraire Jacques Doucet, *fonds* Picabia.

d'un oeil} (Trumpet Call to Awaken the Good Old King of the Monkeys {who only ever sleeps with one eye shut}), for two trumpets in C.

1922

January	*A Table* (The Table), text for *l'Almanach de Cocagne pour l'An 1922*.
January	*Pensée pour* Fanfare (A Thought for *Fanfare*), text for the review of that name.
[January?]	*Choeur des Marins* (The Sailors' Chorus), excerpt from the comic opera *Paul et Virginie*, with libretto by Jean Cocteau and Raymond Radiguet, for tenor, chorus and piano.

> *The Melody and its accompaniment will give each other body.*
> *Light, very raised and sparkling like champagne, is what the music must be like for* Paul & Virginie.[53]

January	*Préambule* (Preamble), talk introducing a concert by Marcelle Meyer and Berthe Albert.
February	*Chronique Musicale: Les "Six"* (Musical Chronicle: "Les Six") for *les feuilles libres*.
March	*Bouquinerie* (Book-loving), text for *Catalogue* published by the Librairie Pierre Trémois.
April	*De la Lecture* (On Reading), text for *Catalogue*.
April	*Office de la Domesticité* (The Servants' Pantry) and *Cahiers d'un Mammifère {extraits}* (A Mammal's Notebooks {Extracts}), for *Le Coeur à Barbe*.
May	*Edition* (Publishing), text for *Catalogue*.
June	*Un très vieil Homme de Lettres* (A very old Man of Letters), text for *Catalogue*.
June-July	*Chronique Musicale: l'Origine d'Instruction* (Musical Chronicle: Educational Background), for *les feuilles libres*.

AVRIL 1922
LE CŒUR A BARBE
1 Fr. JOURNAL TRANSPARENT
Administration: AU SANS PAREIL
37, Avenue Kléber - PARIS (XVIᵉ)
Ont Collaboré à ce 1ᵉʳ numéro:
Paul ELUARD, Th. FRAENKEL, Vincent HUIDOBRO, Mathew JOSEPHSON, Benjamin PÉRET, Georges RIBEMONT-DESSAIGNES, Erik SATIE, SERNER, Rrose SÉLAVY, Philippe SOUPAULT, Tristan TZARA.

---

53. In the margin of sketches for the manuscript score. Private collection.

July	*Igor Strawinsky*, text for *Vanity Fair*.
August	*Claude Debussy*, text for *Vanity Fair*.
October	*Pénibles Exemples* (Bad Examples), text for *Catalogue*.
October–November	*Chronique Musicale: Propos à propos d'Igor Strawinsky* (Musical Chronicle: Points to the Point about Igor Strawinsky), for *les feuilles libres*.
November	*Changement de Saison* (A Change of Season), text for *Catalogue*.
[November?]	*Bonne Education* (Good Upbringing), text for *Catalogue*.

1923

January	*Le Pou qui grimpe* (The Climbing Louse), text introducing a group of painters from Coutances, in Normandy.
March–April	*Chronique Musicale: Les Périmés* (Musical Chronicle: Past their Best), for *les feuilles libres*.
"28th March"	*Tenture de Cabinet préfectoral* (Wall-hanging for a Prefect's Study), "Furniture Music for Mme Eugene Meyer Jr," for small ensemble.
"5th May"	*Ludions*, poems by Léon-Paul Fargue, for voice and piano (or organ).

I. *Air du Rat* (The Rat's Tune). II. *Spleen*. III. *La Grenouille américaine* (The American Frog). IV. *Air du Poète* (The Poet's Tune). V. *Chanson du Chat* (The Cat's Song).

The Rat: funny. Spleen: melancholy. Amewican: fantasmagoria. Papua: light. The Cat: burlesque.[54]

"30th May"	*La Statue retrouvée*, *"divertissement"* (The Statue found, "Diversion"), after an idea by Jean Cocteau, choreography by Leonid Massine, for organ and trumpet in C.

The good old organ is not necessarily religious and funereal. Isn't it a citizen's organ that we find at those lovely gilded fairground rides? Wouldn't you say?[55]

14th June	*Quelques jeunes musiciens* (Some Young Musicians), lecture for the Cercle International des Etudiants, at the Collège de France.

54. In the margin of sketches for the manuscript score. BNF-MUS., MS 9594.

The *"grenouille améouicaine"* (Amewican Frog) is a send-up of misunderstandings and mispronunciations of the well-known *"grenouille armoricaine"* — a recipe originating from the Côte d'Armor in Brittany.

55. Letter to the Comtesse de Beaumont, 26 Dec. 1922, cf. O. Volta, 1989, p.161.

July	*Le Roi de la Grande Ile un grand repas donnait* (The King of the Big Island Gave a Big Meal), for voice and piano.
September-October	*Chronique Musicale: Propos à propos: Parlons à voix basse* (Musical Chronicle: Points to the Point: Let's talk under ourbreath), for *les feuilles libres*.
August-December	*Le Médécin malgré lui*, music for the recitatives of Charles Gounod's opera, libretto by Jules Barbier and Michel Carré, for voice and orchestra, or voice and piano.

> *I am writing Gounod as if it was raining it...*[56]
> *...which is no sillier than writing Ravel.*[57]

1924

January-February	*Mémoires d'un Amnésique: Recoins de ma vie* (Memoirs of an Amnesic: Hidden Corners of My Life), for *les feuilles libres*.
February	*Cahiers d'un Mammifère {extraits de malt}* (A Mammal's Notebooks {Malt Extracts}), for *Création*.
5th February	*Ballets Russes à Monte-Carlo*, text for *Paris-Journal*.
5th March	*L'Esprit Musical* (Musical Spirit), talk for *La Lanterne sourde*, in Brussels.
March-May	*Mercure*, "plastic poses" by Pablo Picasso, in three parts and thirteen tableaux, from an idea by the Comte de Beaumont, choreography by Leonid Massine, for orchestra or piano.

> *These poses are exactly like the ones you can see in any fairground. This show is akin to Music-hall, as it comes without stylisation, and on no account has any connection with art things.*[58]

June	*Cahiers d'un Mammifère {extrait})* (A Mammal's Notebooks {extracts}), for *391*.

---

56. Letter to Darius Milhaud, 19 Aug. 1923. Archives Darius Milhaud.
57. Letter to Igor Strawinsky, 15 Sept 1923. Paul Sacher Stiftung, Fonds Igor Stravinsky, Basle.
58. Interview by Pierre de Massot, *Paris-Journal*, 30 May 1924.

July   *Cahiers d'un Mammifère {extraits}* (A Mammal's Notebooks {extracts}), for
                            391.

July- "October"   *Relâche*, "instantaneist ballet in two acts, one cinematographical interval,
                            and the dog's tail," with theme, curtain, sets and costumes by Francis
                            Picabia, from an idea by Blaise Cendrars, cinematography by René Clair,
                            choreography by Jean Börlin, for orchestra, or piano.

> *The music to "Relâche"? In it I depict*
> *characters who "loaf about." For this reason, I have used popular themes.*
> *These themes are strongly "evocative"... Yes: very "evocative." One could even*
> *say "special."*
> *The "scrupulous" & other "moralists" will reproach me for using these*
> *themes. I have no need to concern myself with such people's opinions...*
> *...Reactionary "blockheads" will issue their fulminations. Bah!... I tolerate only*
> *one judge: the public. They will recognise these themes and not be shocked in any*
> *way to hear them... Are they not "human"?*
> *...I would not wish to make a lobster blush, nor an egg.*
> *Anyone who fears these "evocations" should keep away:...*
> *I should be ashamed to trouble the calm smooth waters of their serene candour...*
> *I am too good-natured to wish to displease them.*[59]

"November"   *Cinéma*, symphonic interval for *Relâche*, for the film *Entr'acte* (Interval) by
                            René Clair, for orchestra (see over).

November   *Cahiers d'un Mammifère {extraits}* (A Mammal's Notebooks {extracts}), for
                            Le Mouvement accéléré.

---

59. La Danse, Nov.-Dec. 1924, page on *Erik Satie.*

The end of Entr'acte, *by René Clair, November 1924.*

GILLMOR, ALAN M., *Erik Satie*, G. K. Hall & Co., Boston, 1988; W. W. Norton, New York & London, 1992.

HARDING, JAMES, *Erik Satie*, Secker & Warburg, London, 1975.

MYERS, ROLLO H., *Erik Satie*, Denis Dobson, London, 1948; Dover, New York, 1968.

ORLEDGE, ROBERT, *Satie the Composer*, Cambridge University Press, 1990 & 1994.

ORLEDGE, ROBERT, *Satie Remembered*, Faber & Faber, London & Boston, 1995.

PAOLA, TOMIE DE, *Bonjour, Mr. Satie*, Putnams, New York; & Hutchinson, London, 1991.

PERLOFF, NANCY, *Art and Everyday: Popular Entertainment and the Circle of Erik Satie*, Clarendon Press, Oxford, 1991.

SHATTUCK, ROGER, *The Banquet Years: Alfred Jarry, Henri Rousseau, Erik Satie, Guillaume Apollinaire*, Random House, Toronto, 1958; Faber & Faber, London, 1959, Alfred A. Knopf, a Vintage book, New York, 1968.

SATIE, ERIK, *Dried Embryos*, translated by Trevor Winkfield, Aloes Books, London, 1972

SATIE, ERIK, *Memoirs of an Amnesiac*, translated by Max Paddison, Recommended Records, London, 1981.

TEMPLIER, P.-D., *Erik Satie*, Paris, 1932, trans. Elena & David French, MIT Press, Cambridge, Mass. & London, 1969.

VOLTA, ORNELLA, *Satie Seen through his Letters*, trans. Michael Bullock, introduced by John Cage, Marion Boyars, London & New York, 1989 & 1994.

WILKINS, NIGEL (ed.), *The Writings of Erik Satie*, Eulenburg, London, 1980. Withdrawn from sale in 1985 after court action by the Erik Satie Estate.

THE ARKHIVE SERIES

In print

1. Dada Berlin

The Dada Almanac, edited by Richard Huelsenbeck, Berlin 1920. Translated, introduced and annotated by Malcolm Green. 176 pp. £13.99 (UK), $19.99 (USA). An important anthology of Dadaist texts assembled by the Berlin Group in 1920. *This version of the Almanac is a crucial document for anyone interested in the 20th century avant-garde. — New York Times Book Review.*

2. French Symbolist and Decadent Writing of the 1890s

The Book of Masks, based upon the collection by Remy de Gourmont, Paris, 1895 and 1896. Translated, edited and introduced by Andrew Mangravite. 304 pp. £13.99 (UK), $19.99 (USA). The largest ever collection of Symbolist writing in English, based around de Gourmont's definitive essays on the movement. *Just the thing to give a neurasthenic idler for Christmas. —The Guardian.*

3. Georges Bataille & Acéphale

Encyclopædia Acephalica, two collections edited by Georges Bataille, and by Robert Lebel & Isabelle Waldberg. Assembled and introduced by Alastair Brotchie. 176 pp. £12.99 (UK), $19.99 (USA). Two anthologies of aggressive texts by the Acéphale and Surrealists groups that take the form of encyclopaedias. *A fascinating instance of the use of cultural forms against culture itself.* — Michael du Plessis in *The American Book Review.*

4. Fluxus/Nouveau Réalisme

An Anecdoted Topography of Chance, by Daniel Spoerri with Robert Filliou, Emmett Williams and Dieter Roth, illustrated by Topor. 240 pp., £14.99 (UK), $24.99 (USA). The latest version of a continuous work. *One of the great books of the century, a comic masterpiece.* — Richard Hamilton in *The Spectator.*

The next two issues:

6. The Oulipo & Ouxpos

Oulipo Compendium, edited by Harry Mathews & Alastair Brotchie, with extensive sections by the Oupeinpo and the Oulipopo and shorter sections by the other "Ouxpos." 240 pp. approx. A definitive collection of the methods employed by the Oulipo and other similar groups, with a major selection of their works.

7. The Vienna Actionists

Direct Art: Blood, Orgies, Mysteries, edited by Malcolm Green in collaboration with the artists. Manifestos, action scripts, handbills, posters and photographic documentation by Günter Brus, Otto Mühl, Herman Nitsch & Rudolf Schwarzkogler. 192 pp. approx.

For a free catalogue listing all our publications (many being for sale by direct mail order only) write to:

BCM ATLAS PRESS, 27 OLD GLOUCESTER STREET, LONDON WC1N 3XX